CREATING
A PACKED HOUSE

10 KEYS TO UNLOCKING
RESTAURANT $UCCESS

BY: A. GLEE ZUMBRENNEN

A Packed House

Picture this: The Beacon Restaurant is nestled in a bustling neighborhood. As you approach, you notice a line of eager diners outside. The exterior is inviting, with attractive landscaping and lighting. The well-lit parking area ensures safety. Large windows reveal a "packed house," with every table and bar area occupied.

Inside, the host warmly greets your party with a "Welcome to the Beacon." Ambient lighting highlights the stylish, impressive decor, blending modern and rustic elements with captivating artwork on the walls. Despite the crowd, the lobby feels cozy and welcoming, with comfortable seating.

Laughter and conversation fill the air, creating a lively ambiance. The busy wait staff is attentive and friendly, expertly navigating through tables with trays of delicious dishes. The open kitchen showcases chefs busily preparing meals with flair.

You are warmly greeted with "Welcome to the Beacon." After a short wait, you're quickly seated, and the menu offers a tantalizing mix of flavors. Beautifully plated food and an impressive drinks menu catch your eye. Your experienced waiter helps with ordering and making thoughtful suggestions. Your orders are correct and served promptly. Your friends comment on how much they enjoy their food. Despite the packed house, the service is efficient, and the staff handles the busy environment with professionalism, ensuring each guest feels valued.

The room's energy is infectious, making your dining experience unforgettable. The "packed house" vibe enhances the enjoyment, making it about more than just the food— it's the people, ambiance, and shared excitement that make it special and magical.

"A restaurant has as many guests as it can satisfy."

"Where is the person who sincerely aims at excellence in music, painting, literature, or in any trade, business, or profession who is not willing to give their whole life to the acquirement of that particular perfection?" "They who, deep in their heart, adore truth, and aspire to know it, will consider no labor too great to be undertaken, but will adopt it joyfully and pursue it patiently."

–James Allen - philosophical writer 1864-1912

DEDICATION

This book is dedicated to the thousands of young people who have worked at Brick Oven Restaurant over the past 50+ years. They are, without a doubt, the finest group of people one could have the opportunity to work with. They have made the Brick Oven Restaurant what it is today, and many are our heroes. We have learned much from associating with them.

Our heroes are those who consistently and tirelessly provided "Loven from the Oven." They exhibited "The Spirit of Brick Oven" while bringing guests back time and time again. They have performed ordinary work extraordinarily well.

Our best product has been "Loven from the Oven." It's what we did, meeting the needs and wants of our employees and guests; it's what keeps them coming back. Creating "Loven from the Oven"

It has been the driving force and spirit of literally thousands of employees. It's made up of many small things: a smile, a friendly welcome, a thank you, a clean restroom, steamy hot delicious food, a clean saltshaker, a highchair or window, fast service, eye contact, a clean dish, a pat on the back, a welcome to Brick Oven and so much more.

Consider the manager who can't sleep because a customer's order was late last night; the baker who starts at 6:00 a.m. to make doughs; the host who remains cheery after greeting a thousand guests in a crowded lobby; the driver who delivers orders in a rainstorm and smiles at the customer's door; the custodian who cheerfully cleans up carpet stains; the cook who works next to a hot oven for hours, never complaining about special rush order requests; the pasta chef who serves an endless line of hungry guests; the server who stays cheerful when serving a large party arriving right at closing time and ensures the guest with a special food request gets precisely what they want; the crew that works shorthanded when someone is sick; the salad bar assistant who keeps the bar looking great during a full house; the cashier who spends extra time at the end of a busy night balancing the till to the penny; and the dishwasher who washes dishes continuously for eight hours. The list goes on and on, year after year.

Going the extra mile to create "Loven from the Oven" adds meaning to the job and fosters personal growth. It enables an employee to practice being their best. No effort is ever wasted.

Thank you, Heroes.

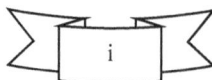

"Although the skills aren't hard to learn, finding the happiness and finding the satisfaction and finding fulfillment in continuously serving somebody else something good to eat, is what makes a really good restaurant."

–Mario Batali - American chef, writer, restaurateur, and media personality

Always a packed house . . . that's how you know.

"Brick Oven is a wonderful place to eat. The price is right, the food is delicious, and the service is fast and personable. I've been eating there for 27 years and it's still an amazing place. It's a staple for anyone who has ever attended BYU or lives in Provo."

–Missjenny54 - Trip Advisors

WHAT READERS SAY

"I was amazed how complete your book is. It's filled with operational info as well as a great read. It will give wonderful insight to current operators as well as start-ups."

–Glen A. Overton – Hotelier and Ruth's Chris Restaurant franchisee.

"Glee Zumbrennen, is an icon in Utah Valley, his experience and knowledge of the restaurant business drips from every page. His willingness to share all he has learned shows up in the details of this book. Pay attention to the systems he has created, and it will help you succeed. Good Luck"

–Richard Parkinson – Owner of Magleby's and Magleby's Fresh restaurants.

"Wow! My initial impressions are extremely positive: you have really delved deeper than any similar book I have seen, offering many practical ideas and tips in every chapter. I really like the ten tips or principles and how you have beefed them up with real tips not just fluff."

–Kevin R. Miller, Author of *Customers Only Want Two Things,* Consultant, and President of Vision Bound International.

"A treasure trove of insights from someone who has seen it all. A must-read for anyone seeking long-term success in the restaurant business. I am a very satisfied 50-year customer of Heaps of Pizza –Brick Oven Restaurant."

–David M.R. Covey, Author of *Trap Tales-Outsmarting The 7 Hidden Obstacles to Success.*

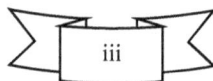

TABLE OF CONTENTS

INTRODUCTION

TEN PROVEN KEYS FOR RESTAURANT SUCCESS

I operated a "Packed House" restaurant. Our restaurant was full during lunch and dinner hours; most every day we were open. After over fifty years of working for and thinking about the guests, I discovered the keys to restaurant success. I tried to determine everything Guests wanted from their restaurant experience. Even if you have a packed restaurant, you have work to do if you're not making a good profit. Profit is the essential ingredient to your future success.

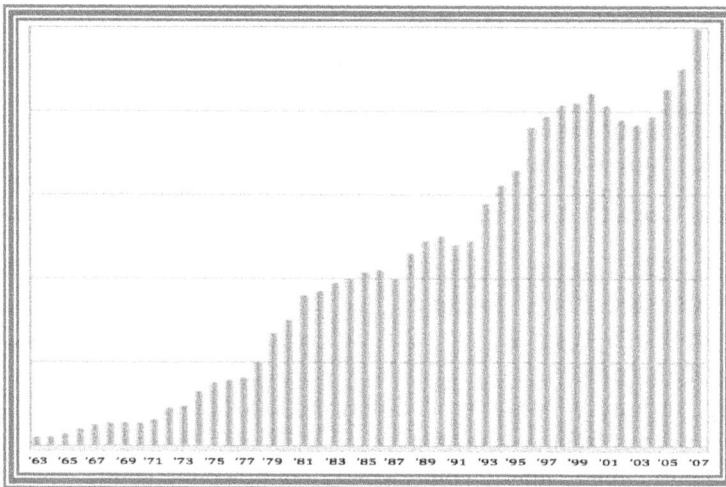

Our annual sales graph from 1963 until 2007

Overcoming Challenges

Over forty-six years, we experienced five years of sales decrease. Each time, I diligently worked to uncover the reasons behind our shortcomings in execution or guest experience. The chapters in this book will guide you in improving your restaurant's operations and ensuring sustained growth.

Understanding Your Guests

This book answers crucial questions about restaurant guests: what they want, how to increase their patronage, why they choose or avoid certain restaurants, and the number

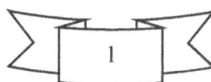

one reason restaurants fail. It explains how we built a successful restaurant in a conservative market, increasing sales fifty-fold over 46 years.

Striving for Excellence

Making your restaurant the best in its field is a formidable challenge. Can you be the best on your block, in your town, state, or even the nation? How far can you go? This book is designed to help you achieve excellence by focusing on every detail of your restaurant business and maintaining high standards consistently, day in and day out, month after month.

KEYS TO SUCCESS - PROFIT OR GUEST ENJOYMENT?

This book is divided into sections detailing the ten keys to your success. *This book highlights the importance of minimizing your risk of operating a restaurant.* This boils down to avoiding losing your customers or guests, as I like to call them. Not only is it essential to provide a wonderful experience, but it is also equally important to avoid subjecting them to things that will discourage them from coming back. Over emphasizing profit over your guest's enjoyment is a dangerous position and can lead to a loss of business (fewer customers). You can approach the business for profit or guests' enjoyment. I strongly suggest choosing guest's enjoyment every time they visit your restaurant. Neven ever can you get complacent about your guests' enjoyment. There is a subtle difference between the two. When emphasizing profit, there is a tendency or temptation to cut corners to increase profits by reducing costs.

Overcoming Operational Challenges

Operating a restaurant requires overcoming many challenges like facility wear and tear, evolving market needs, staff turnover, and managing staff trends. Despite some of these obstacles, our success was due to focusing on guest satisfaction and creating an environment where guests and staff thrived.

Practical Guide to Success

This book emphasizes the importance of guest enjoyment in determining success and provides a practical guide to achieving growing sales and profitability. Details matter, and this book outlines key principles for:

Total guest enjoyment

Effective staff management

Systematizing your operations

Profitability of your restaurant

Yours's and your staff's personal growth

General business operating ideas

Purpose of the Book

This book aims to educate restaurant owners and managers, helping them manage to overcome everyday operational challenges and succeed. It focuses on developing and refining the management skills of owners and managers so their staff can maintain facilities and prepare and serve food to guests in a manner that provides unique enjoyment—while ensuring profitability. Many principles of this book are repeated in various sections to emphasize their importance.

OPENING A NEW RESTAURANT CHECKLIST

Operating a restaurant is about the management of staff members. I can be immensely rewarding, especially in serving others. It can also be profitable and prestigious, like being the host of the town. However, it requires significant effort, involves stress, and carries risks. This book focuses on minimizing the risks associated with operating a restaurant. Every step you take to organize your business better reduces the chances of failure. There are many factors involved in the restaurant industry. Here is a list of ten key projects to guide you in opening a restaurant.

TEN STEPS TO OPENING A RESTAURANT

1. Survey the Market and Write a Business Plan

Create a business plan to address important questions and prepare for the journey ahead. Your business plan should include:

Company overview and description

Executive summary

Market analysis

Business offering

Management strengths

Marketing strategies

Financial projections

The business plan will help you plan your restaurant and can also be presented to potential investors or lenders for funding evaluation. Determine a feasible trading area that aligns with your concept. Identify your primary customers: families, singles, students, or businesspeople. Understand their dining preferences and unmet needs in the trading area.

Conduct a thorough market survey within about 5 miles of your proposed location to understand what people in the area want in a restaurant. Engage with potential customers to learn about their preferences for food, beverage, service style, décor, atmosphere, and price. Plot your actual trading area on a map, as well as your maximum trading area.

Avoid the mistake of creating a restaurant based on your personal preferences rather than the desires of your target market. Your family and a few friends may not represent the broader market's wants, so avoid relying solely on them for your commitment. Survey a wide range of people to understand their preferences for food products, facilities, services, pricing, and potential frequency of visits.

Today's customers seek a complete restaurant experience and value community and cultural support, as well as sustainable practices. Your restaurant concept should be unique, offering clear value and differentiation in the marketplace. Identify any unmet needs in your trading area and plot the demographic concentration of your target customers on a map. Consider available marketing strategies to reach your audience effectively.

2. Defining Your Restaurant Concept and Assessing Market Viability

After carefully defining your restaurant concept, ensure that the population within your trading area (3 to 5-mile radius of your location) includes enough of your target market customers. Your target customers could be families with children, business executives, millennials, college students, and so forth.

Once you complete a thorough trading area survey, you'll be ready to develop your main menu items and their corresponding recipes and preparation methods. These items will form the core of your restaurant and should appeal to as many impartial people as possible. Research the best ingredients that will make your menu items stand out from similar offerings in the marketplace, and document detailed recipes and production processes for every menu item. Additionally, determine the number and type of staff members, inventory, and equipment you will need to start the business. Every aspect must be well thought out, designed, and constructed before you open the restaurant. Listen to your market and let them tell you what they want.

Next, evaluate the financial feasibility of your restaurant concept. The annual total sales of your restaurant should be approximately 1.5 times the total investment. If your idea cannot realistically achieve this sales volume at a proposed location, it might not be a viable project. For example, if your total investment is expected to be $750,000, you should aim for annual sales of about $1.2 to $1.5 million. Estimate the sales volume by multiplying the predicted check average by the number of guests you can reasonably expect on an average day. Then multiply this figure by the number of days your restaurant will be open during the year.

3. Develop the Name and Logo of Your Restaurant

Your restaurant's name and logo should encapsulate the essence of the food, service, and ambiance you intend to offer. Ideally, people should get an idea of your restaurant's concept just by looking at its name and logo. To achieve this, hire a skilled graphic artist to create a visually appealing logo.

A compelling name and captivating logo can entice potential customers and spark their curiosity about your dishes and drinks even before they step inside. Your name should align with your restaurant's brand and reinforce its identity. Effective branding encompasses everything from your restaurant name and logo to the colors and fonts used on menus and advertisements.

Choosing the Right Name

Uniqueness: Your restaurant's name should be distinctive and one-of-a-kind. Ensure it is not already trademarked or used by another business in your state.

Memorability: Opt for a name that is easy to remember. Avoid long, complicated, or generic names that might be forgettable.

Descriptiveness: Select a name that clearly conveys the type of restaurant you are developing. Consider incorporating words like restaurant, café, bistro, bar, diner, eatery, or another unique descriptor that fits your concept.

By thoughtfully developing your restaurant's name and logo, you set the stage for a cohesive and appealing brand that resonates with your target audience and makes a lasting impression.

4. Secure an Ideal Physical Location for Your Restaurant

Leasing a building in the perfect location for your restaurant is crucial. It's wise to avoid building a new structure before proving your restaurant concept is profitable. A knowledgeable commercial real estate agent can help you find suitable locations and navigate local zoning laws that dictate where restaurants can operate. Your location should be in an area with a significant number of your target customers, be highly visible, have convenient access from traffic routes, and offer ample parking.

Your occupancy costs should not exceed 10% of your projected sales to ensure profitability. These costs include rent, property taxes, insurance, and common area expenses. For instance, if your annual occupancy costs are $70,000, you need to be confident that your annual sales will be at least $700,000. High rent can jeopardize your restaurant's success and profitability.

Design the physical layout of your restaurant efficiently, including the dining area, kitchen, storage, break rooms, and offices. Plan the equipment, tables, utensils, guest seating arrangements, entrance and greeting facilities, and restrooms in great detail. Consider the design and décor of your restaurant's menu, signage, and overall facilities.

Hiring a professional design company, lighting, and décor experts can be a worthwhile investment. They can plan your building's interior and exterior to communicate your brand image to your guests effectively. Restaurant supply companies can assist in designing kitchen and dining room layouts, as well as recommend seating, equipment, supplies, and signage.

5. Establish a Relationship with Food Suppliers

Building strong relationships with food suppliers is crucial for your restaurant's success. Start by obtaining vendor price quotes to determine the best suppliers for each food and beverage ingredient for your menu items. Keep in mind that pricing varies across different product categories, and competitive bidding can help you secure the best deals.

Think of buying food like purchasing a car—vendors often charge what the market will bear, so it's essential to negotiate and shop around. Smaller-volume restaurants typically face higher prices, but effective purchasing strategies can significantly impact your restaurant's profitability and your supplies, beverage, and food costs.

6. Detail All Administrative, Production, and Service Jobs with Written Systems

Decide whether your restaurant will be full service, fast casual, or fast food. Analyze your competition to understand their strengths and identify the advantages you will have over them.

Create comprehensive employee manuals, general operating rules and values, forms, checklists, and specific job methods and procedures to train your managers and staff members. Develop clear instructions that govern how your employees will work together to serve your guests. Determine the necessary skills for each staff position and outline the methods you will use to train them. People are the most critical asset in your restaurant operation, so selecting the right individuals to produce and deliver your products and services is crucial.

Develop written systems that include your vision, values, mission statement, policies, and checklists to guide the restaurant's daily operations. Remember, failure to plan is planning to fail.

Define your company's values, mission, vision, and motto to inspire your staff. Create detailed standards and operating conditions to provide clear guidance on your objectives and big-picture goals.

Implement solid financial controls to safeguard cash, liquor, supplies, and inventory. With a large staff, there are numerous ways to lose money in the restaurant business. A lack of controls can lead to excessive waste, spoilage, and theft.

7. Hire a Business Accountant and Attorney

An attorney is crucial for forming a business entity, whether it's a sole proprietorship, partnership, corporation, or LLC. They will review all legal documents you need to sign, providing essential guidance when signing leases and other contracts.

An experienced and competent accountant is vital for maintaining accurate financial records, understanding your restaurant's finances, and filing tax returns. They will help ensure your financial health and compliance.

Additionally, a good banker can assist with financial matters such as cash requirements, loans, and capital needs. They will serve as a reliable financial resource and provide convenient banking services for deposits and payments to suppliers and creditors. Your business plan will be necessary to your bank when establishing a line of credit for your restaurant.

Keep in mind that cost estimates for opening your restaurant may be lower than actual costs due to unforeseen expenses and time delays during construction and installation. Plan for a cushion of 20% additional investment cash to cover unexpected contingencies and cost overruns. This ensures you won't be undercapitalized and run out of cash before your restaurant has a chance to become profitable.

8. Register with the Local, State, and Federal Government for Tax ID Purposes

Ensure compliance by registering with the local, state, and federal government to obtain your tax identification number—secure permission to operate by applying for a business license from the appropriate city authorities. Additionally, arrange for utility hookups by making necessary deposits for electricity, water, sewer, natural gas, and high-speed internet services.

9. Hire and Train a Qualified Staff

This step includes recruiting management, supervisors, and staff members who will help bring your restaurant vision to life. Determine competitive pay scales for both management positions and front- and back-of-house roles. Remember, the restaurant industry is all about people—delivering a memorable experience, not just a great meal. Hiring exceptional front-of-house staff who respect quality customer service is critical, as they will represent your restaurant in their interactions with guests.

While opening a restaurant, you may be tempted to "hire in haste" to expedite the process. Resist this urge. Instead, create a structured hiring plan that includes pre-written job descriptions for quick online posting, pre-set interview questions, and a thorough vetting process. Always check references, and be prepared to read between the lines, as many employers tend to give favorable recommendations to former employees.

The range of staff required will depend on the type of restaurant you own. Ensure thorough training for your staff, preparing them to serve your first guests in a way that impresses them and encourages repeat visits. Carefully select and thoroughly train your team members to minimize turnover, which is essential for consistent and efficient operations. Your restaurant management should avoid being overly controlling; today's employees need an inspiring leader to be effective and productive.

10. Select a Marketing Company with the Skills to Help You Develop a Unique Strategy

Hire a skilled marketing company to create a unique strategy for your restaurant. They can help you design and print a comprehensive menu showcasing your food and beverage offerings. Your total food costs are crucial to your success and should be between 20-35% of total sales. Menu prices determine your total food cost and must reflect value to your guests. Aim to have no more than 7-10 items per category of appetizers, mains, sides, and desserts. Your ideal prime costs (food and labor) should be under 60% of sales.

Develop a marketing strategy and website for publicity, public announcements, advertising, and promotion of your restaurant. The final step in opening a restaurant is launching your external marketing plan. Begin marketing about a month before your opening and have your strategy for the entire year ready before officially opening your doors. *I recommend focusing on attraction rather than promotion for long-term success.*

OPEN YOUR RESTAURANT WITH EXCELLENT EXECUTION

Ensure your restaurant's grand opening is a success by focusing on delivering delicious products, fast and friendly service, impeccable cleanliness, and an inviting ambiance and décor. Your staff must operate at peak efficiency from the moment your doors open to the public.

All operating systems must be fully functional well before opening day. Ensure that all food recipes are written so that every meal is prepared consistently every time. Many new restaurants fail due to an overwhelming influx of curious customers, so it's essential to be prepared.

Consider hosting a soft opening for a limited number of guests before your official opening. This "test run" allows you to identify areas where your staff can improve efficiency and effectiveness during specific mealtimes. Initially, you may need to hire additional staff to allow time for developing the necessary skills and coordination.

A RESTAURANT CAN BE A SAIL OR AN ANCHOR FOR ITS OWNERS

This book aims to help make your restaurant a sail that propels you forward rather than an anchor that holds you back financially by reducing the inherent risks of restaurant ownership.

After discussing your restaurant's mission, values, purpose, promise, standards, systems, rules, and practices, the most crucial factor is management. Everything hinges on excellent management. If your management is ineffective and allows staff to do as they please, you will struggle to succeed. A restaurant must be meticulously managed from the front of the house to the back. Without a well-thought-out plan, your restaurant is likely to fail. Guests have high expectations and will not tolerate mediocre food, facilities, or service. Ineffective management leads to a frustrating and costly restaurant experience. I believe that "any restaurant can be successful." The difference lies in management.

The key to operating a successful restaurant, once a viable concept is developed in a suitable market, is effective operation. To operate effectively, you need to execute a detailed, well-thought-out plan for serving your guests. This requires effective management of your staff. While you can hire experienced managers and delegate operations to them, this is risky because not all experienced managers are good managers. Many ineffective restaurant managers have substantial experience. Experience can be beneficial or detrimental. Entrusting your restaurant to the wrong management can ruin its potential for success.

Walt Disney said it best.

"We will do what we do so well that the people who see it will want to see it again and bring friends."

THE #1 REASON RESTAURANTS FAIL

Inexperienced and unskilled owners, managers, and staff members making critical mistakes in maintaining facilities, preparing food, and serving guests can lead to a poor guest experience and financial disaster. Allowing staff members to prepare and serve food to guests the way the staff members think is satisfactory is the cause of most restaurant failures.

There are many reasons a once-successful restaurant might fail. Some contributing factors include:

Management Changes: Selling the restaurant or losing effective management can lead to a decline in operational standards. Signs like "Under New Management" or "New Owner" often indicate attempts to regain customer trust after such decreases.

Market Changes: Loss of sales due to shifts in market demographics or accessibility, such as customers moving away, losing their jobs, or changes in parking availability. The surrounding market area may also deteriorate or change, affecting the restaurant's primary customer base.

Outdated Concept: Failing to evolve with the times, leading to outdated facilities, décor, menu offerings, or service styles that no longer appeal to the changing market demographics.

Food Safety Incidents: Publicized food poisoning incidents can severely damage a restaurant's reputation.

A restaurant's long-term success hinges on building a loyal customer base and maintaining profitability. Success can be elusive due to the high turnover of staff and management, highlighting the need for effective hiring, training, and management practices.

Other Potential Issues Include

Lack of Integrity and Maturity: Staff members may engage in dishonest behaviors such as buddy punching, wasting time, or stealing cash and materials. They might be unhappy or disgruntled for various reasons.

Lack of Commitment: Staff may lack good work ethics, stamina, and understanding of what constitutes a fair day's work for a fair day's pay.

Indifference to Guests: Staff members may display an attitude of indifference toward guests, be distracted by social needs, or fail to prioritize their work responsibilities. Excessive chatting, flirting, and cellphone use can detract from guest satisfaction.

Inexperience: Young or inexperienced staff may lack the skills needed to meet guest expectations or be productive enough for the restaurant to be profitable. Issues with punctuality, personal hygiene, respect for guests and coworkers, and poor communication skills can further exacerbate these problems.

Managing these risks requires strong leadership, clear communication, and a commitment to maintaining high standards across all aspects of the restaurant's operation.

Managers may allow staff members to do their jobs without addressing the potential staff member shortcomings listed above. They may have many of the characteristics and weaknesses of their staff members listed above. They may be inclined to be a pal manager needing friendships more than the respect of a successfully run operation. They may lack practical leadership skills. They may give staff members the freedom to do their work the way the staff members want at the expense of the Guest's experience. They may not be aware of the operational style and methods being used by their subordinates.

Lack of Integrity and Work Ethic: Managers may falsify sales records, embezzle cash and materials, or give away food to friends and family. They might waste time instead of managing staff on the floor.

Lack of Motivation and Experience: Managers might misuse their position, fail to appreciate good work, and treat employees harshly. They may not understand financial statements or cost control, and they might neglect cleanliness, safety, and quality service.

Inadequate Hiring and Training Skills: Managers may not prioritize hiring, training, or supervising staff effectively. They might avoid demanding excellent performance and lack experience in leading staff positively.

Lack of Commitment: Managers may be more interested in owning their own restaurant or be dissatisfied with their pay and job requirements.

Owners' Operational Knowledge Gaps: Owners might not fully understand restaurant operations or staff and management shortcomings. They may underestimate the risks of running a restaurant and fail to implement secure procedures to prevent theft and dishonesty. They may also be uninvolved, relying entirely on management, and not compensate staff adequately to ensure high performance.

Lack of Effective Management Experience: Owners may lack a good business plan and fail to clearly define the restaurant's theme, mission, values, service style, and food preparation techniques. They might not prioritize sanitation, cleanliness, and safety or recognize the importance of written operating systems. They may also lack cost control knowledge, delegation skills, and practical training for management and staff.

Time Constraints: Owners may not have enough time to address managerial and staff shortcomings, especially if the restaurant is their secondary occupation. They might lack effective leadership skills.

Lack of Business Acumen: Owners may not realize the challenges of operating a restaurant and managing staff. They may be motivated by the idea of being the "host of the town" without understanding what it takes to succeed. They might lack interest in the operational details, leading to issues such as an overly extensive and confusing menu, inventory overspending, spoilage, waste, and insufficient financial capacity to achieve profitability.

They may have misjudged cost overruns, unforeseen expenses, and delays associated with opening a restaurant. Overspending on furniture and ambiance can deplete resources before achieving profitability.

Ignorance is bliss.

"Ignorance is not bliss. Ignorance is poverty. Ignorance is devastation. Ignorance is tragedy. And ignorance is illness. It all stems from ignorance."

"Failure is not a single, cataclysmic event. You don't fail overnight. Instead, failure is a few errors in judgement repeated every day."

"A formal education will make you a living, self-education will make you a fortune."

–Jim Rohn - Entrepreneur, author, motivational speaker

FIRST KEY TO $UCCESS
IDENTIFY AND UNDERSTAND YOUR GUESTS

"Nothing is so powerful as an insight into human nature . . .what compulsions drive a man; what instincts dominate his actions. . . if you know these things about a man you can touch him at the core of his being."

–William Bernbach

SETTING THE STAGE - KNOWING YOUR GUESTS

It is true that all people are different and have varying needs, preferences, and tastes. You satisfy almost everyone by choosing to meet the most discriminating guests with the highest standards, expectations, and need for value. Develop the skill of listening, talking to, and surveying your guests to determine precisely what they want from your restaurant. Discovering their likes and dislikes can be a challenge, but much of it is common sense if you think about it. The answers to the questions presented here about your guests aim to help you set high standards and understand "what makes most people tick."

Guests who are made to feel like an inconvenience or a burden will seek another restaurant. Competitors are ready and willing to take any underserved guests. Winning in the restaurant business is not a game of chance. The answers to the following questions are some of the essential underlying rules of winning the restaurant game. When you understand these rules, you have the advantage because most of your competitors don't. Understand your guests' hospitality requirements to know what it takes to retain them. Understanding and "reading" the needs of guests is almost an art form, requiring discernment and observation of who they are, even by age group, income level, and social status.

ANSWERING THESE QUESTIONS ABOUT YOUR GUESTS

What Do Guests Want Most from a Restaurant?

How Do You Increase a Guest's Patronage?

What Are People's Needs?

How Do People Choose a Restaurant?

What Do Restaurant Guests Hate?

What Do Guests Notice About a Restaurant?

Why Don't Guests Come Back?

What Do Guests Appreciate?

Why Do People Eat Out?

What Are Restaurant Guests Looking For?

What Do Guests Hide?

What Do Guests Want Most from a Restaurant?

"Restaurant guests require much more than just a meal; they seek an enjoyable experience above all else, or they will look for it among your competitors."

The word "restaurant" originates from the French word *"restaurer,"* meaning *"to restore or refresh."* Guests' enjoyment requires meticulous attention to detail, from attractive ingredients and flavors to overall ambiance. Guests won't explicitly demand enjoyment; instead, they will quietly take their business elsewhere if their expectations aren't met. If you fail to provide cleanliness, friendliness, delicious food, and fast service, guests will seek out other establishments that do, taking their money with them. Your primary focus must be on understanding and meeting the requirements of your guests for an exceptional dining experience. Nothing can replace this dedicated attention.

Most people have limited funds and will choose restaurants where they get the most value for their money. They expect fair prices, excellent service, delicious food, a pleasant atmosphere, and cleanliness. When their expectations are not met, they feel cheated and disappointed.

Running a restaurant involves numerous projects, problems, tasks, and undertakings that constantly vie for your attention. These can easily divert your focus from guests and consume your time. Responsibilities such as hiring, training, evaluating staff members, addressing personal issues, repairing and maintaining facilities, attending management meetings, handling insurance coverage, complying with government regulations and inspections, making license and tax payments, creating advertising and promotional materials, and more, can become full-time tasks if not appropriately managed.

How Do You Increase a Guest's Patronage?

"The more enjoyment a guest receives from a restaurant experience, the more often they will return."

Transform the essential act of eating into a ritual that involves hospitality, imagination, satisfaction, graciousness, and warmth. Elevate a basic human need into a sophisticated pleasure. When a restaurant operates consistently at a high level, it should see significant sales growth year after year. The more value and enjoyment you provide your guests, the more often they will visit. The sweeter the experience, the more attractive your restaurant becomes, leading to higher sales and greater profits through controlled expenses.

Unconscious needs and emotions drive guest choices. You've heard the sayings, "You can't buy love" or "You can't buy happiness." While these may be true, people continuously seek fulfillment through their choices. Emotions are powerful motivators for purchasing decisions. Think about the last appliance, article of clothing, vehicle, or service you bought. What were you indeed after? Convenience, looking good, feeling good, solving a problem? Major companies' advertising often taps into these emotions and needs.

There are three potential outcomes for a guest's restaurant experience:

They experience a net positive, enjoyable experience, increasing their desire to return.

They experience a net neutral experience, meaning their desire to return remains unchanged.

They have a net negative experience, leading to a decreased desire to return, whether consciously or subconsciously. This can cause them to forget your restaurant and remove it from their list of dining options.

Effective management is crucial to creating positive guest experiences. Managers must ensure guests have the experiences they intend by overseeing staff adherence to established methods, procedures, and systems. The general manager or owner must act as the guest's representative, ensuring that all aspects of the restaurant meet the highest standards.

The general manager must be familiar with every job system and able to observe cleanliness, room and food temperatures, maintenance, and tidiness. They must also ensure the accuracy and timeliness of service and the quality of food. By being free from production duties, managers can observe and correct deficiencies and commend the staff for their work, thus guaranteeing procedural execution and guest satisfaction.

If your systems are designed to provide guest satisfaction, you only need to ensure they are followed and are the best possible systems. There is no need to ask guests how they enjoyed their experience if you have guest-satisfying procedures in place. Inquiries can be for conversation or to double-check procedural execution.

As an owner or manager, it's essential to know what your staff should be doing and ensure they are doing it effectively.

"I have never wished to cater to the crowd; for what I know they do not approve, and what they approve I do not know."

–Epicurus (341-270 BC)

Listen to Guests Carefully to Discover Their Needs. Listening to guests can be done in many ways:

Face-to-face conversations, listening to suggestions and compliments.

Reading guest comment cards that are conveniently placed for guests to report on their experience.

Conducting periodic focus groups with your key guests.

Gathering insights from staff members who hear occasional guest comments.

Reading rare letters or notes from guests about their experiences.

Studying the results of surveys and studies about your guests' experiences.

Reflecting on your own experiences when dining at your restaurant or a competitor's.

Listening to friends and family who share their dining out experiences.

All these methods can help you understand what your guests genuinely value in a restaurant experience. Guests are generally reluctant to complain directly to staff or managers, so any feedback you receive is valuable.

Dissatisfaction with how a food item is prepared or guests may perceive a service performed as an intentional change by your restaurant. To guests, the operation of a restaurant seems straightforward, so they often assume any change in food or service is deliberate.

Complaints are opportunities. Just as problems are opportunities in disguise, so are guest complaints. When guests complain, they are trying to tell you what they want! If you don't listen and make changes, your competitors may attract them away from you. Guests not only prefer enjoyment; ultimately, they require it and will find it elsewhere if needed.

Don't dismiss guests who complain as more trouble than they're worth. Instead, listen to them. Understand their point of view, seek opportunities to improve your business, and retain them as loyal guests. Their experience likely mirrors that of others, and at the very least, you may learn something valuable.

Value is more important than price. Everyone wants a good deal, but people seek value for their money rather than mere bargains. By emphasizing good service and improved products, you differentiate your restaurant positively from the competition. If your restaurant's perceived value is genuinely better, guests will be happy and won't mind moderately higher prices. An old rule of thumb is that if you raise prices by 1%, you lose 1% of your customers.

"People choose to patronize a restaurant because their image of it is better than their image of competing restaurants."

People select a restaurant based on their perception of the enjoyment they receive. Competing restaurants vie for patrons by creating compelling images of enjoyment in people's minds. Each person forms an enjoyment image of a restaurant, and the one with the most potent positive image wins their patronage. Guests expect enjoyment in exchange for their money.

Never let your staff set service standards themselves. Some staff members might assume guests come solely to eat and that their job is done once the food is served. This misconception has led many restaurants to lose clientele and close. Your guests require much more from a dining experience. Please work with your staff to set the highest practical standards and take control of your guests' experience by understanding their needs. If you don't define the planned guest experience, your staff will.

Strive to create a strong enjoyment image for your restaurant by delivering a series of enjoyable stimuli through what guests see, hear, touch, and experience from your staff. Their experience begins the moment they first hear about your restaurant, see your building, or see an advertisement. These impressions continue as they observe the exterior, landscape, and parking lot, feel the friendliness of the host and servers, hear pleasant sounds, taste and see the food and beverages, and feel the cleanliness of the table and seating.

Throughout their visit, guests accumulate positive and negative experiences. Their conscious and subconscious minds tally the total enjoyment minus any discomforts they encounter. This perceived value forms their image of your restaurant.

What Do Restaurant Guests Hate?

"People Like Order, Reliability and Consistency. People Hate Chaos."

"O Consistency, Consistency, Thou Art A Jewel" is a well-known quote sometimes ascribed to William Shakespeare. Whether or not it originated with him isn't nearly as important as the reality that consistency can be a jewel when it comes to your ability to persuade people to return to your restaurant.

Choosing Consistency Vs. Chaos/In the Weeds

In his book *12 Rules for Life,* Jordan Peterson defines chaos.

"Chaos is the despair and horror you feel when you have been profoundly betrayed. It's the place you end up when things fall apart; when your dreams die, your career collapses, or your marriage ends. It's the underworld of fairytales and myth, where the dragon and the gold it guards eternally co-exist. Chaos is where we are when we don't know where we are, and what we are doing when we don't know what we are doing. It is, in short, all those things and situations we neither know nor understand."

Chaos arises when any aspect of a restaurant experience is not correctly cared for. In a restaurant, chaos manifests as inconsistency, unreliability, delays, lack of a service plan, discomfort, irritation, uncertainty, strangeness, unfriendliness, neglect, disrepair, lack of attention to detail, poor manners, and unpleasant sights, noises, or smells. Unexpected events that are not anticipated or handled promptly add further chaos for your guests.

Facilities are in chaos when they are unattractive, dirty, cluttered, in disrepair, broken, stained, or have uncomfortable temperatures. Service is in chaos when guests experience delays in seating, order-taking, food delivery, or check presentation. Indifferent, distracted, unfriendly, inattentive, or poorly dressed staff contribute to guests' perception of chaos.

Jordan Peterson further defines order as the opposite of chaos.

"Order is the floor beneath your feet, and your plan for the day. It's the greatness of tradition, the rows of desks in a school classroom, the trains that leave on time, the calendar, and the clock.   Order is the public façade we're called upon to wear, the politeness of a gathering of civilized strangers, and the thin ice on which we all skate. Order is the place where the behavior of the world matches your expectations and your desires; the place where all things turn out the way we want them to."

ORDER IN A RESTAURANT

Order in a restaurant means that all aspects of the dining experience are consistently and reliably attended to, ensuring guest satisfaction. Order exists when the restaurant's methods foster a welcoming feeling, certainty, timeliness, structure, well-executed plans, consistency, reliability, friendliness, familiarity, peace, comfort, cleanliness, attention to detail, and attractiveness. Unexpected events are anticipated and handled promptly.

Guests perceive the condition of various factors within your restaurant and interpret what that means for their experience. When your staff cares for guests and ensures a pleasant experience, it is evident. Conversely, if your staff appears indifferent or unwilling to provide a satisfactory experience, guests will notice.

All restaurant guests have experienced chaos at some point—long lines, delays, forgotten orders, uncomfortable temperatures, poorly prepared food, wrong orders, confusion, and frustration. They are quick to recognize these signs and dislike them intensely.

People value consistency and reliability. They feel uncomfortable when subjected to chaos or inconsistency. Generally, people strive to minimize chaos and create order in their daily lives. The saying "O Consistency, Consistency thou art a jewel" applies significantly to the restaurant business.

What Do Guests Notice About a Restaurant?

"Guests perceive every detail in their restaurant experience."

You can't hide anything from guests. Their perception of your restaurant is shaped by what they hear, smell, taste, feel, and see. This perception becomes their reality and influences their future dining choices, determining whether or not your restaurant's name will be considered for future visits. If you don't perceive everything that happens in your restaurant, you'll be at a disadvantage, as your guests will know more about your operation than you do.

"There is a limit to what can be held in a person's conscious focal awareness, an alternative storehouse of one's knowledge and prior experience is needed, which we label the subconscious."

–Locke and Kristof

Your Guests' Unconscious Mind

The experiences your guests have at your restaurant are both conscious and unconscious. People store unconscious events in their memory just as they do conscious ones. These unconscious events shape your guests' image of your restaurant and influence how likely they are to return. In other words, your guests see, feel, taste, hear, and smell everything, even if they don't consciously acknowledge it. Every detail about your restaurant is critical, even if you aren't aware of its importance.

Your challenge is to become aware of everything your guests notice and ensure every aspect of your restaurant is positive and attractive in their minds. Both conscious and unconscious experiences form a potential guest's image of your restaurant.

The unconscious mind plays a more significant role than we think in making dining decisions. Perception is reality. What guests perceive, whether correct or not, is fundamental to them. The unconscious mind is emotional and irrational, seeking gratification and being influenced by the way products and services make us feel. Purchasing decisions, including where to dine, are made by the unconscious mind, with the conscious mind later justifying the choice.

If your unconscious mind notices everything about your experiences, it might know more than your conscious mind about your previous dining experiences. Therefore, it's crucial to pay attention to the details of your guests' experiences and ensure they are positive and attractive.

You can control what guests see, smell, taste, hear, and feel. Operate based on attraction rather than promotion. By creating enjoyment for your guests, you can build loyalty and encourage them to speak well of your restaurant. Satisfied guests will return often and promote your restaurant through word-of-mouth. Word of mouth should be the essence of your marketing strategy. Dissatisfied guests, on the other hand, will share their negative experiences with others. A lesser-known fact is that "96% of unhappy guests won't complain to you but will tell 15 friends."

"It's what you don't know that hurts you, only you won't know it."

–The Mind Verses the Senses, from Wenzel's Menu Maker by George Leonard Wenzel, January 1, 1964

THE POWER OF THE SENSES

All desires are emotional feelings stimulated in the brain by messages carried by the various senses through the different nerves. The brain then reacts automatically by referring to memories of previous similar or closely related experiences. It sends response commands through the different nerves to the eyes, ears, noses, mouths, and hands. What is called a 'conditioned reflex' is a shortcut caused by repeated sensory experiences that form a 'memory path' or what is known as a 'habit.' A fly that lights on a horse causes the tail to swish without the horse thinking about it instantly. Two or three experiences with a badly smelling order of fried shrimp cause a customer to turn up his nose at the mention of the restaurant at fault.

A restaurant deals more with the human senses than it does with people as whole units. Its contact with the public has no intellectual, moral, or religious overtones, and it makes it easier for the alert manager to deal directly with the specific sensory organs to create prejudices in favor of or against your establishment.

Only Three Effects

Each and every restaurant customer leaves with one of three impressions:

1. They may develop a desire to come back again.

2. Or they are left with a feeling of total indifference.

3. Or they have stored an abhorrent feeling for you, the food, one or more of the staff members, or something about the place or service.

The degree to which you exert yourself in involving the public's five senses most satisfactorily will be the measure of your success as a suitor in their favor. Contrariwise, the degree to which you repulse the public with disagreeable effects on the eye, ear, nose, mouth, and hand will mark your restaurant down as one of those places to avoid.

The Eye-*The eye is by far the most powerful of the senses. It can detect the difference in a shade of color varying only one 1/millionth! For most things, the eye has a sensitivity of $1/100^{th}$.*

The Tongue-*The tongue can detect $1/200,000^{th}$ part of an acid. That means it can detect the presence of one-part quinine in $200,000^{th}$ parts of water. The tongue is sensitive to $1/200^{th}$ difference in the taste of sugar presence. It is sensitive to five taste stimuli: sweet, sour, bitter, salty, and salty-bitter like Epsom salts. Coffee is not a taste. It is an odor we detect as we swallow and force the aroma up our nose.*

The Nose-*The nose can pick out the odor of musk if only $1/32, 500^{th}$ part is present. We have here a powerful stimulant, which can be used to create 'odor memories' that will make an indelible impression in the minds of your Guests.*

The Ear-*The least sensitive of all the organs is the ear, which requires one gun to be a third louder than another before the ear can detect any sound difference. A great deal of your sensitivity to hearing depends upon the attitude of the hearer.*

The Hand-*The hand is the least sensitive in that it can detect only 1/20th of the weight difference. Thus, if one article weighs 20 pounds, a second would have to weigh either 19 or 21 pounds before a person could tell the difference.*

To set your restaurant apart from competitors, you must provide guests with enjoyable sounds, tastes, smells, sights, and tactile experiences. By satisfying all five senses, you create a memorable and delightful experience for your guests, ensuring they return again and again.

Why Don't Guests Come Back?

"68% Of Surveyed Guests That Don't Come Back To A Restaurant Say It Was Because They Encountered An 'Attitude Of Indifference.'"

Indifference is the trait of remaining calm and seeming not to care; it reflects a casual concern, nonchalance, and a carefree attitude—essentially, a lack of worry or responsibility. Indifferent people can appear cold, aloof, disinterested, unmotivated, and lacking in passion. It's crucial to ensure that your staff members do not fall into a state of indifference.

"Certain drugs such as marijuana and narcotics may cause people to be indifferent. People can also be apathetic because of illnesses such as depression or other brain disorders. However, there may be a more insidious cause.

There is good evidence that people are gradually becoming more narcissistic. We find a growing sense of selfishness in the world. Our pride and unrestrained egos cause us to place ourselves first and everybody else a far second. The result of this self-indulgence is that we are indifferent to everything else that may be going on around us. We end up not caring about the suffering of others."

–Ken Buckle -- The Psychology of Indifference

It's easy for staff members to be momentarily distracted by personal concerns or others and lapse into indifference. Remaining focused requires concentration on the task of pleasing guests, mainly when many guests do not communicate their displeasure.

Guests must be re-sold on your restaurant every time they visit. You must go beyond merely feeding people. You need to attract guests back often by creating a magnetic appeal around your restaurant. Consistently providing excellent services, food, and facilities that exceed guest enjoyment expectations is crucial. Survival in the highly competitive restaurant industry is impossible without a strong attraction.

Every interaction with a guest, whether by phone or in person, is a combination of positive and negative impressions. Your job is to minimize or eliminate negative impressions and maximize positive ones to encourage guests to return.

14% of guests say they became dissatisfied with the restaurant's operation.

9% leave for competitive reasons, which you can do little about.

5% develop new interests or friends.

3% move out of the area.

1% die.

Each guest contact is a risk and an opportunity. Your commitment to providing consistently excellent service and experiences is what will keep guests coming back and speaking positively about your restaurant.

Experiences that Restaurant Guests Might Perceive as Staff Indifference

When staff members prioritize personal conversations, phone calls, or personal indulgences such as eating, drinking, or grooming in view of guests.

When there is a delay in being seated for a reservation.

When a restaurant is understaffed and "in the weeds."

When a service need is neglected, such as slow food service, delayed clearing of used dishes, slow presentation of the guest check, and slow meal payment collection.

When food is not prepared correctly.

When guests encounter unnecessary delays.

When mistakes occur and there is no apology from the staff.

When a guest's need is neglected, and they feel that nobody shows concern.

When a guest has a question, and nobody is available to answer it.

When the dining experience is poorly coordinated.

When guests perceive the restaurant's facilities are neglected, such as issues with cleanliness, sanitation, safety, clutter, or facility repairs.

When there is a delay in answering telephone calls or when placing a customer on hold.

"We know what a person thinks not when he tells us what he thinks, but by his actions."

–Isaac Bashevis Singer, a Polish American writer in Yiddish.

Don't Wake Your Loyal Guests Up with a Poor Experience

People are creatures of habit. Loyal guests are those who, when they have a need, automatically think of a specific business. They are in love with that business. It could be a dentist, a website, a barber or hair stylist, a brokerage firm, a tree surgeon, a hardware store, a plumber, a grocery store, or a restaurant. They have developed comfortable traditions in their spending habits and are content with their past patronage decisions. They never consider alternatives when they need a service or product that a particular business consistently provides.

The decision-making process about which business to use is initially challenging. It requires evaluating alternatives, location, pricing, selection, service level, friendliness, consistency, reliability, quality, and all the other attributes they seek in a business. People prefer not to go through this complex evaluation process to find a new source of satisfaction.

This is why loyal guests can be so upset when their chosen provider disrupts their comfortable habit with an unexpected problem, inconsistency, or an unsatisfactory event or change. For a while, they haven't even considered using another business for their recurring needs.

> *Never let repairs, receiving goods, sales calls, interviews, training etc. interfere with yours and your staff's' focus on guests and their enjoyment during the critical breakfast, lunch and dinner periods.*

When a person is irritated by a problem, they may look for a better solution. The problem could be a new, supposedly improved condition, a change in service consistency, indifference or lack of attention from a staff member, or a price increase. If the customer wakes up and thinks, "Things have changed here enough that I'm going to look around for a better option," they will begin the challenging process of replacing the provider. What was once a solid number one choice might fall behind as the person finds a new favorite that offers the same comfort and ease they once enjoyed.

This is why it is crucial that your restaurant experience remains consistent and reliable in service and product quality day in and day out. Keep your guests happy and content to prevent them from looking for an alternative restaurant. Don't wake your contented guests up.

GUESTS REQUIRE ACTIVE MANAGEMENT

The restaurant business is fundamentally a hospitality business, and focusing on guests must be a priority. You invite prospective guests into your restaurant to provide them with nourishment and comfort. They deserve your staff's total respect and consideration. Referring to them as "guests" rather than "customers" underscores their importance.

Guest relations are paramount in any business, especially in the restaurant industry. Guests are the ones who pay your wages and all the bills; they are genuinely the bosses. With all the efforts that go on in a restaurant, it's easy to forget the importance of the guest.

Consider the advantages of being overzealous about guest enjoyment and the possibility that only the paranoid survives. Being fanatical about guest satisfaction prevents complacency in guest service. For example, Bill Gates was paranoid about Microsoft losing market share to competition. By being overzealous, you can satisfy even the most demanding guests, which in turn means satisfying all your guests.

Keep Your Restaurant's Name in the Hat

An adage says that "to choose someone as the winner of a competition in which everyone has an equal chance of winning is often done by taking a name written on a piece of paper out of a hat." Keep your name in your guests' minds—out of sight, out of mind." Very rarely do people toss a coin to decide which restaurant they will patronize; there's too much at risk. The risk of being disappointed is accurate for most people who have had poor experiences with restaurants. Unless the images of the restaurants being considered are valued equally by each person, a coin toss is not an option.

The restaurant industry is notoriously tricky. You've likely heard the frequently quoted adage that most new restaurants don't make it past the first year.

To emphasize the potential influence of events and conditions on guests, think of adverse events that happen to a guest in a restaurant as suffering because that is what a poor experience creates for them.

"Nothing is so powerful as an insight into human nature . . . what compulsions drive a man, what instincts dominate his actions, if you know these things about a man you can touch him at the core of his being."

–William Bernbach, founder of Doyle-Dane-Bernbach Advertising Agency

Consequences of Taking Care of Guests

Understand that guests are the source of your success and job security, embodying the promise that "When you take care of guests, they take care of you." Reflect on why you wanted to be an operator or manager. Is it to learn how to serve guests through the work of others successfully? Is it for higher pay, status, progress, security, more responsibility, or self-improvement? The guests are powerful—they are your ultimate employers, providing your paycheck, profits, and future.

Guests look for someone they can count on to champion their point of view and ensure they are always taken care of. They need someone who:

Understands them and knows how they feel and what they expect.

Knows their tastes and what pleases them.

Makes decisions with their interests in mind.

Ensures they are treated in a friendly manner.

Makes them feel welcome and appreciated.

They can always depend on.

Stands up for them in the face of competing needs.

Guests will seek out someone who:

Sympathizes with their wants and needs.

Discovers better ways to create enjoyment for them.

Defends them against suffering an unenjoyable experience and mistreatment (being ignored, stalled, or neglected).

What Do Restaurant Guests Appreciate?

"The Main thing people appreciate in a restaurant

is a staff that takes care of their restaurant needs."

Guests appreciate management and staff someone who:

Eliminates unpleasant or uncomfortable conditions, such as irritations, distasteful food, dirty conditions, facilities in disrepair, and delays.

Saves them time by providing fast food and service.

Ensures they have enjoyable experiences.

Provides delicious foods quickly, with pleasant sounds, smells, and attractive sights.

Gives them the most value for their money.

Makes their life easier.

Makes them feel important and appreciated.

In return, the guest will:

Provide you with personal success and opportunities.

Identify you as a winner, standing out in a crowd of competitors.

Consider you a friend and a resource.

Promote you into more responsible positions that will protect you against economic cycles and the uncertainty of changing business conditions.

Provide you with financial security through reliable wages, higher salary, and above-average retirement income.

Offer you positions of responsibility, more challenging work, a higher lifestyle, and a brighter future.

Earn you the recognition and respect of your family, friends, and neighbors.

Cause others to esteem and think highly of you.

Grant you status in your community and neighborhood.

Offer you positions of trust and authority, with respect from others as they recognize your success.

Provide you opportunities to grow and expand your restaurant.

These opportunities can easily be achieved if you respect the power of your guests to provide.

Distractions That Can Keep You from Focusing on Guests

Why all the emphasis on the guest? Isn't it common knowledge that the object of every business is to satisfy the customer? While the adage "the customer is always right" is well-known, there are countless distractions in the restaurant business that can divert focus from guests.

Operating a restaurant involves:

Managing staff members

Meeting with vendors for purchasing and receiving food and supplies

Conducting staff training and management meetings

Managing accounts payable and taxes

Undergoing health department inspections and complying with government regulations

Maintaining equipment and dealing with breakdowns

Addressing facility issues

Overseeing food production

Handling advertising and media

Participating in community service

These tasks, among others, can easily distract you from focusing on your guests.

At times, your staff members may not prioritize guests over their personal needs. They may lack financial interest in or experience with running a successful restaurant operation. It's crucial to have motivated management present to encourage staff members to maintain focus on guests.

Mere slogans and pronouncements are insufficient and quickly forgotten in the daily bustle of the restaurant business. Real effort and concentration are required to remember guests every day and in every situation, despite other responsibilities. Guests have an advantage over your staff; they have complete awareness and nothing to do but carefully observe their dining experience.

Once, I received a blistering complaint from a customer who felt neglected while dining with a large group of 20 guests at our restaurant. I decided to visit her home to apologize. After listening to her complaints, I apologized and asked her to request a manager if she ever had a problem in our restaurant again. She responded that there had been a manager in the dining room at the time who did nothing about the poor service. She said, "The manager should have been more aware of what was going on."

Unless you have a self-service or counter operation where customers partially manage their orders, management needs to keep staff members focused on providing a great guest experience.

A RESTAURANT CAN BE TWO DIFFERENT WORLDS

At times, a restaurant can feel like it consists of two different worlds. One is the world of the guest, which is the most important and the one we all agree should be prioritized. The other is the world of the staff. This dynamic is similar to the relationship between pedestrians and automobile drivers at a crosswalk. The pedestrian believes they have the right of way and the car should stop. The driver acknowledges this but thinks it would be easier for the pedestrian to pause for five seconds so the car can pass.

Each side has its point of view, believing their perspective is the most important. This creates an invisible wall between guests and staff. In practice, staff members or even management may rationalize prioritizing their own views slightly. It's easy for staff to ignore guests momentarily by finishing personal conversations, prioritizing side work, taking a quick break, checking their work schedule, or being casual instead of hustling to serve guests.

Management's perspective is different; it is like a pilot's view from above, overseeing the entire operation. Managers need to see service priorities and situations that require immediate attention. They must watch both sides of the invisible wall and direct staff members when necessary to ensure all guests receive the best possible service. Assuming that all guests are being served expeditiously and promptly is a dangerous assumption if you intend to guarantee great service.

"If you're looking to have a future in the restaurant industry the first thing you learn is that you have to care for Guests. You can talk about margins and locations and a lot of other things, but if you don't take care of your guests, you don't have a future in restaurants."

–Carl Karcher, Founder of Carl's Jr. restaurants

WHY DO PEOPLE EAT OUT?

"The Main Reason People Eat Out Is to Nurture Relationships."

Eating Out is a Social Experience

Eating out is an opportunity to have a shared dining experience. Guests primarily seek the emotional gratification of associating together while enjoying a meal. A guest-driven restaurant operator ignites staff enthusiasm and vigor in serving guests. Strive to understand guests and their inner thoughts while sharpening your job skills to satisfy more people.

Understand and provide for guests' emotional needs. Guests visit restaurants for many reasons beyond eating. They seek social interactions, conduct business, celebrate, meet new people, and spend time with family, friends, or business associates. Facilitate a pleasant experience without distractions like a soiled, cluttered facility, slow service, order mistakes, or poor-quality food. The primary need a restaurant fulfills is social.

People need to build, maintain, or renew relationships. This is what is meant by "People do not go out to eat; they eat to go out." You are not just providing food; you are creating an enjoyable dining experience where guests build and strengthen relationships and celebrate special occasions.

Pay passionate attention to details. Providing great service is a state of mind. While errors are inevitable, you can significantly reduce losses in guest enjoyment through meticulous attention to detail. Communicate the importance of details to your staff, demonstrating your passion for guest service through your example and insistence on guest satisfaction. Good service should be prompt and unobtrusive, allowing guests to enjoy their conversations without unnecessary interruptions. Mature servers will know when interaction is welcomed and when it's a distraction.

Keep your staff focused on exceeding guest enjoyment requirements. This focus and care create an environment where guests feel comfortable and valued. Such a climate makes guests more understanding of occasional mistakes or delays. If your heart is dedicated to following your systems, an occasional mistake will not lose a guest's confidence or lessen your restaurant's image. Staff interests may not always align with guest interests. If guests enjoy their experience, they'll return often. If they don't, they won't. Therefore, keep your staff on the right track by influencing them to perform quality work according to your systems efficiently and consistently.

What are Restaurant Guests Looking for?

"Restaurant guests are looking for new tastes and new amenity experiences, as well as enjoying consistent old favorites."

As a restaurant operator, you must continuously explore and test new tastes and amenity experiences. The expectations for quality products and services are continually rising. New amenities and products multiply at an accelerated pace. Continuously develop new and better products, faster and friendlier service systems, and more interesting amenities and décor to enhance your guests' enjoyment.

The foodservice landscape is ever-changing. Some trendy food items and practices endure for a long time, while others fade quickly. Always look for the latest trends in flavors, spices, foods, cooking methods, and presentations that fit your operation and could become popular with your guests.

Examples of current trends in the restaurant business as taken from the National Restaurant Association's latest *What's Hot* article.

"Many major quick service restaurant companies have added a plant-based protein or a meat alternative to the menu in 2019. Experts expect plant-based protein food products will continue to grow in popularity during the next decade."

"Sustainable choices: More than half of consumers say they are likely to make a restaurant choice based on its eco-friendly practices, such as water conservation, packaging and recycling.

"Top overall trends in 2020 are: Healthy bowls, Scratch made items, Creativity with catering, specialty burger blends and unique beef and pork cuts."

What Do Guests Hide?

"Guests generally conceal their true feelings about an unpleasant restaurant experience from the staff."

Surveys have shown that 96% of guests experiencing a problem do not complain. A mistake or delay is a problem even if guests do not comment. Therefore, it is essential to recognize, apologize for, and correct food and beverage mistakes and service delays as they occur. Guests need to know you are aware of a problem and are addressing it. This perception of high standards gives them confidence in your ability to provide fast, error-free products and services in the future. Treat all guest problems from their perspective and offer immediate, thorough responses to their remarks and complaints.

Many guests don't tell you when they are disappointed. They don't want to be perceived as unreasonable or demanding. They often hide negative feelings and pay their check with a smile, sometimes even looking you in the eye and saying, "Everything is OK," despite having had a problem. Many guests even smile and tip after poor service to avoid creating an awkward situation or getting someone in trouble. This usually leads to guests leaving without expressing dissatisfaction, depriving the restaurant management of valuable feedback.

Because guests often remain silent about negative experiences, it can fool you into thinking they are satisfied. This makes it easy for your staff to slip into neutral attitudes, slow service, inconsistent products, and poorly maintained facilities without realizing there is a problem.

Many guests are uncomfortable complaining to management or staff but will share their negative experiences with an average of eleven other people. For every complaint you receive, there are likely twenty-five other unhappy guests who don't complain. This means that for every twenty-five unhappy guests, about 275 potential guests are warned to avoid your restaurant. Staff members often don't relay guest complaints to management, thinking they aren't necessary.

"Although the skills aren't hard to learn, finding the happiness and finding the satisfaction and finding fulfillment in continuously serving somebody else something good to eat, is what makes a really good restaurant.

–Mario Batali.

Forty Examples of What Can Disappoint Guests

When guests cannot find a convenient parking place.

When the restaurant opens late or closes early, despite posted regular hours.

When they are not greeted with a smile, hello, or eye contact.

When they are not seated immediately despite seeing empty tables.

When they are made to feel like an inconvenience or interruption.

When the tabletop is not thoroughly cleaned or picture-perfect.

When chairs and booths have crumbs on them.

When tables and chairs are wobbly or placed too close to walls or other tables.

When they are ready to order, and their server is not available.

When the restaurant runs out of a menu item.

When lettuce salads are not cold, crisp, or are rusted.

When their water glasses are not automatically refilled.

When hot food is not served hot, and cold food is served at room temperature.

When the phone rings more than three times before being answered.

When they are put on hold for more than 30 seconds.

When dishes or glasses are chipped.

When their silverware is spotted or has food particles on it.

When glasses are streaked (hold them up to light, and you might be shocked).

When food is slow to be served from the kitchen.

When salad bars are messy and lack visual appeal.

When prepared food sits in the service window, waiting to be picked up.

When salt, pepper, and other condiment shakers are greasy to the touch.

When a server's apron looks like a cook's after a busy shift.

When a staff member has an "I am doing you a favor

" attitude.

When soft drinks come out of the system flat or weak.

When debris, paper, and food are not picked up from the floors.

When they order based on the menu description but receive something else.

When they are told delivery will take 30 minutes, but it takes 60 minutes.

When their meal garnish is limp and dried out.

When sticky or dirty rags are used to wipe down tables.

When they are on a tight schedule and cannot get in and out of the restaurant quickly.

When dirty dishes are left on their table for too long.

When they have to look at a table of dirty dishes next to them.

When restrooms are not spotlessly clean and well-stocked.

When they see staff talking together instead of attending to their needs.

When it takes longer than 10 minutes for a to-go order.

When a complaint is not handled to their satisfaction.

When they are not thanked and invited back.

When a special request is not fulfilled.

When a staff member touches a glass, straw, or fork where guests put their mouth.

"Dining Guests having had a poor experience, responding to 'how was everything,' generally says fine."

"If you work just for money, you'll never make it, but if you love what you're doing and always put the customer first, success will be yours."

–Ray Krock, founder of McDonalds corporation.

A Guest Requirement for Enjoyment Statement

"I am used to being surprised and delighted with many things. I am hard to impress. I have high expectations. I value my money greatly and don't spend it easily. I require a lot in return when I buy something. I am continuously looking for something better. If I am disappointed with the experience I have at a restaurant, I will remember it for a long time and warn many others about it. If I am surprised at how wonderful my experience is, I will be back and will tell a few others about it.

Everything I see, hear, smell, or touch must favorably impress me. This includes your advertising, your vehicles, what others say about you, the neighborhood in which you are located—absolutely everything. My impression of a restaurant consists of the people who work there, whether they are on or off duty.

The first thing I require is a sanitary and clean restaurant. I will not come to your restaurant if I feel I may contract a disease or come into contact with germs. I must be convinced by what I see that you handle your food carefully so I am not going to get sick or contract food poisoning. You must keep the restrooms looking clean and smelling fresh and sanitary.

I require a spotlessly clean restaurant and this includes everything, starting from the parking lot, the landscape, and walkways. I want to feel like I am the only person using your restrooms. I do not like to see any evidence that others have used your facilities before me.

Don't let me see fingerprints, dust, smudges, crumbs, litter, worn surfaces, broken equipment, or evidence that others used my table.

If you can surprise me and attract me back by providing cleaner facilities, more smartly dressed employees, and sanitary conditions, I will be your loyal customer."

SECOND KEY TO $UCCESS
DESIGN AN ENJOYABLE GUEST EXPERIENCE

"It's the business you create, the absolute uniqueness of being the best in its field. That's what matters."

–Richard Branson

CRAFT YOUR RESTAURANT CONCEPT

Use your creativity and past experiences to develop a comprehensive concept for your restaurant. Imagine the food and beverages: their appearance, taste, portions, textures, and presentation. Consider the look and feel of dishes, glassware, and utensils.

Think about the service style you will offer. Will it be full service, fast casual, quick service, or buffet style? Envision the dining experience from your customers' perspective. Imagine the décor and facilities and how they will appeal to your guests. Consider every detail of the building: parking, entrances, and interior spaces.

Identify your target audience and determine your hours of operation. Analyze your competition. Visualize the detailed experience you will provide your guests. What will it feel like for them to dine in your restaurant?

Developing Your Restaurant's Concept

What is your passion and your concept? Is it something you want to spend your time on every day creating? Test your idea with people in your key market. Are they interested in your restaurant concept? Will it easily support the cuisine and service you are planning? Your concept idea needs to stand out in people's minds as unique and interesting to them. The vibrance of the site, location, food, service, and décor all need to fit together nicely for a successful concept.

Key Considerations

Restaurant Bar: Will your restaurant have a bar? Most restaurant concepts include a liquor bar, which is vital for the restaurant's theme and profitability. In most regions, a bar is an essential element of the restaurant scene. Controlling liquor use is a crucial part of the operation.

Experience Over Items: According to a study by Eventbrite and Harris Interactive, customer spending on experiences has increased by 70% since 1987. The study also shows that 78% of millennials would rather purchase an experience than an item or product. While dinner itself is an experience, unique restaurant themes go the extra mile by adding entertainment.

"Business more than any other occupation is a continual dealing with the future; it is a continual calculation, an instinctive exercise in foresight."

–Henry R Luce, publisher

Picking Your Restaurant's Theme: There are thousands of different restaurant themes, as many as there are restaurants. Restaurants with interesting themes provide unique experiences beyond just dining.

Key Points to Consider

Theme Development: Choose a theme you can develop into an engaging, exciting, and even dramatic décor package. Your restaurant theme should align well with your food offerings and provide a memorable dining experience. The vibrance of the site, location, food, service, and décor should all fit together seamlessly.

Entertainment Component: Dinner itself can be an experience, but unique restaurant themes go the extra mile by adding an entertainment component. This can enhance the overall dining experience and make it more memorable.

Market Appeal: Your theme should be attractive to your target market and make them feel comfortable. It should stand out in people's minds as unique and interesting.

Contribution to Success: An effective theme presentation can significantly contribute to your restaurant's sales volume and, ultimately, financial success.

Questions to Consider

Has your theme been used before, or are you thinking about a new theme?

Do you plan to improve on an existing theme and express it uniquely?

By thoughtfully developing your restaurant's theme, you can create a standout dining experience that keeps guests coming back for more.

RESTAURANT CONCEPT TYPES

Fast Food Concepts: Attract patrons with service speed, drive-thru convenience, and affordable prices.

Fast Casual Concepts: Offer disposable dishes and flatware but present food as more upscale, with gourmet bread and organic ingredients. Open kitchens, where patrons can see their food being prepared, are popular with fast-casual chains.

Casual Family Concepts: Offer moderately priced entrees from menus featuring a mix of classic cuisines, individualized with signature sauces or other toppings. Casual style dining can include Barbecue, Asian, Western, Italian, Americana, or Mexican cuisines. These restaurants offer table-side service in a low-key setting while keeping the menu moderately priced.

Fine Dining Concepts: Offer patrons the finest in food, service, and atmosphere—the highest-priced type of restaurant you can operate.

Bistro Concepts: Do not offer table service. Patrons order their food from drive-thru convenience or a counter and serve themselves. A bistro menu traditionally provides items such as coffee, espresso, pastries, and sandwiches.

Buffet Concepts: Have patrons serve themselves from a variety of dishes set out on tables or bars.

Food Truck Concepts: Feature low cost and low overhead, making them one of the easier ways to open a new restaurant. Another advantage is their mobility, allowing them to go where the patrons are.

Each restaurant concept has its own uniqueness and appeal. Some restaurants can have a combination concept with self-service bar options along with standard full-service. Display cooking can be interesting for guests and give authenticity to the meal preparation process. Many restaurants offer counter service as well as full table service.

EMPATHIZE WITH GUESTS

Empathizing with guests means being aware of their feelings, enjoyment, needs, and concerns. It involves sensing their feelings and perspectives and taking an active interest in them. It requires anticipating, recognizing, and meeting their need for enjoyment, particularly in situations where guests may conceal their true feelings—a common scenario in the restaurant world.

Sensing what others feel without their explicit expression captures the essence of empathy. Guests rarely verbalize their emotions; instead, they communicate through tone, facial expressions, or nonverbal cues. Empathy entails reading and responding to unspoken concerns or feelings. At its highest level, empathy understands the underlying issues or concerns behind someone's feelings, such as the perceived high cost of a meal or worries about food safety.

People with empathy sense others' feelings and perspectives and take an active interest in their concerns. They are attentive to emotional cues, sensitive to guests' prompts and suggestions, and show understanding of guests' perspectives. An empathic person is service-oriented and constantly finds ways to increase guest satisfaction, enjoyment, and loyalty. They offer appropriate assistance, grasp guests' perspectives, and act like a friend. They closely watch guests' reactions while using products and services, see their responses to flavors and textures, and feel their reactions to interactions with staff members. Empathic individuals listen well, going beyond what they hear to ensure they understand—this is active listening.

With empathy, you will be prepared to assist in supervising and deploying systems that meet guests' needs. You will feel frustrated when your guest is frustrated and comfortable when your guest is comfortable. All your operating systems must be designed with empathy towards guests. Their expectations continue to rise with more dining experiences, and they demand increasing satisfaction from the marketplace.

Empathy is "getting inside the skin of the guest" and "making every business decision based on their satisfaction."

CREATE YOUR RESTAURANT'S SENSORY PACKAGE

The objective of your sensory package is to cause your guests to think, "Instantly, something told me that I was in a special place," when entering your restaurant. Your sensory package is a combination of every subtle condition and experience your guests have, whether it be sight, sound, aroma, texture, temperature, or taste. Your company logos should be presented tastefully to brand your products and services. The colors and shapes in your logo, brochures, fliers, advertisements, business cards, and letterhead should always be consistent to convey the same message. Guests should have a history of positive sensory experiences with your restaurant.

How you design your sensory package depends on one thing: your guests. What do they expect from you? What are you going to promise through your sensory package? Remember, you are not marketing to yourself. What appeals to you is not important— what appeals to your guests is.

The combination of sensory input leads to the overall impression your guests get from your restaurant, giving them a reason to choose your establishment. Each environment holds the promise of different emotional gratifications. Knowing what guests are looking for enables you to provide it by building a sensory package targeted to their needs.

The image of your restaurant is the picture created in the minds of your guests and prospective guests, along with the emotional impressions they associate with it. (Remember, even your guests today are prospective guests for tomorrow.) This involves a combination of conscious plus unconscious, reason plus impulse, logic plus emotion. The emotional, impulsive, unconscious part of us holds most of the influence on how people perceive your restaurant. The enjoyment image people have is mainly based on emotional impressions formed through all elements of your sensory package—what they see, hear, smell, taste, and touch. Everything they sense leaves an impression.

Your restaurant's sensory package is the part you can control. The image created by your sensory package is up to each individual. Your job is to craft your sensory package to make the most favorable enjoyment image in the minds of your desired guests, using what you know about their demographics and psychographics.

Consider these four characteristics when choosing shapes and colors for your restaurant:

Visibility: Certain colors and shapes are more easily seen by both the conscious and unconscious minds. Visibility is crucial to attract guests' attention. Some colors and shapes, like yellow, have high visibility, while others, like blue, have low visibility.

Retention: Certain colors and shapes are more easily remembered by the unconscious. High-retention colors and shapes make advertising and the product more enjoyable, recognizable, and memorable.

Preference: Research indicates that some colors and shapes are innately more appealing than others. For example, blue is highly preferred by men in all its shades. Variations of basic shapes have the same preference as the fundamental shape they most resemble. There are only four primary shapes in terms of sensory impact and emotional response: circles, squares, triangles, and ovals.

Association: Every color and shape stimulates the guests' unconscious association with feelings, memories, fantasies, fears, or events. Positive associations attract guests, while negative associations repel them.

Important Restaurant Sensory Package Standards Examples:

Aroma standards: The aroma in and around your building is one of the freshly prepared foods.

The restaurant and particularly the restrooms smell clean without a perfumed smell.

There are no stale, musty, greasy, or soiled smells in or around your restaurant.

The perfume smells on staff members will offend many Guests.

Sight standards: All surfaces are spotlessly clean and in like-new condition. Every place you look is pleasant and appealing.

Avoid workstation visibility. They are impossible to keep clean and organized. Besides, they are not considered attractive. However, they may become part of your restaurant décor.

Tile floors are clean and show no sign of mop marks on the walls. The carpeted floors are of a complimentary color and clean without any sign of wear.

Window glass and mirrors are spotlessly clean.

There's no evidence of excessive wear and tear on any surface.

The facilities are neatly arranged and orderly, with everything in its assigned place.

The colors are bright, and all painted surfaces are well-painted without any checking.

The landscape is attractively manicured and filled with plants and flowers during the growing season.

Lawns are green and healthy without any evidence of wear or drying out.

China glassware condiments are spotlessly clean without signs of wear or chipping.

Dining room tables, chairs, booths, and counters are clean, attractively designed, and well-maintained. Overstuffed seats and cushioned back coverings have no signs of wear or broken springs and cushions.

Light fixtures have no burned-out bulbs and are clean and free of dust.

Wall décor, displays, and signage are bright and dust-free.

Staff are dressed in clean uniforms or clothing and appear ready to receive Guests.

Window treatments are stylish. All fabrics are soft and match the restaurant's theme.

Touch standards: Everything in your restaurant feels clean to the touch.

Menus, condiment containers, chairs and tables feel clean to the Guest's touch.

Handrails and door handles feel clean to the touch.

Buffet plates and glassware feel clean to the touch.

Booths and chairs are comfortable to sit on.

Sound standards: Guests hear pleasant sounds in your restaurant. They hear background pleasant, enjoyable music filling the restaurant to drown out or mute unpleasant sounds or the loud conversations of other Guests.

Guests don't hear unpleasant radio communication between staff members.

Guests never hear power cleaning vacuums, mixers, and other equipment making unpleasant noises.

Kitchen production and other distracting sounds are minimal.

Staff member interaction with Guests is friendly and pleasant.

The table bussing is being done quietly to avoid the clanging of dishes and glassware.

The ceilings have acoustical tile to soften the sounds.

Staff member telephone voices have a smile in them.

Temperature standards: The temperature of the restaurant feels neutral to Guests without any heavy airflow blowing on them. Working staff members may not be comfortable with the same temperatures as Guests.

Hot foods are served hot, and cold foods are served cold.

Feelings standards: Guests *feel* welcome and are treated as if they were VIP royalty by your staff. Your staff members are friendly and outgoing energetic people who smile at people easily.

Your staff members are engaged with Guests trying, in every way, to please them.

Guests *feel* comfortable because your staff members are well-groomed and dressed in spotlessly clean, color-coordinated uniforms.

Guests *feel* bonded to your restaurant in a unique and personal way. Their relationship with your staff is strong and has sealed their loyalty to your restaurant.

"If anything is good for pounding humility into you permanently, it's the restaurant business."

–Anthony Bourdain, American celebrity chef

HOW WELL IS YOUR RESTAURANT DOING?

If you are already in the restaurant business: Make a general observation about your restaurant's facilities, personnel, products, and services from your customer's enjoyment point of view:

Walk around your restaurant. Try to experience it from a guest's perspective. Does the parking, entry, and exterior of the building, dumpster, and receiving porch say "welcome"?

Be a guest in your own restaurant. (Knowing that you might be treated more carefully than a regular guest by your staff.)

What is the overall ambiance and experience you feel? Is it a welcoming, positive atmosphere for guests and staff?

Do the staff members appear to be enjoying their work? How could you be nicer to your staff members? Are your guests enjoying their meal experience?

Conduct a focus group discussion with a few of your typical target guests.

From your guest's perspective, list the best and worst qualities of your restaurant.

Make a list of the things you think could be improved to create a more enjoyable experience and build better relationships with your guests and staff.

How could your staff members be more uniquely friendly to guests?

Talk to your guests and consider asking any of these questions on a written questionnaire, over the phone, or as you come into contact with them in your restaurant:

How well do we deliver what we promise?

How do we compare with our competition?

Was the information about our products and services provided on our menu and signage adequate?

Did we give you the help you needed?

Is the quality of our products and services consistently excellent?

How do we rate in dealing with your complaints on a timely basis? Are we willing to address any special needs you may have?

Have you ever had an unsatisfactory experience with our restaurant? Was it resolved in a timely and satisfactory manner?

Are our staff members friendly, attentive, courteous, responsive, and well-trained?

What could we do to make your experience excellent?

Do our services and products meet your needs?

What additional or related products or services would you be interested in?

What could we do to provide a more personalized, unique service to you?

Based on the results of seeing your business through the eyes of your guests, assessing your competition, thinking about your own experience, and talking to your guests, generate a list of new facility, food, and service opportunities for your restaurant. Don't hold back. Don't judge or evaluate the ideas at this point. Let your creative juices flow and come up with as many ideas as you can for adding services or products to your restaurant.

Check Out Your Competition

Be a guest in their restaurant and make general observations about your experience:

Does their staff appear to be enjoying their work?

Do their guests seem to be enjoying their meal experience?

From their guests' perspective, list the best and worst qualities of their restaurant.

What things do you do better than your competition? What do they do better than you?

Why do their guests patronize them? Ambiance? Menu selection? Service processes?

Ask your server what their best-selling menu items are.

List things you learned from your competition.

"In every instance, we found that the best-run companies stay as close to their customers as humanly possible."

–Thomas J Peters, business writer

An Enjoyable Dining Experience

"A clear picture of what we are trying to create together."

We wanted to go to a restaurant to enjoy some pleasant socializing together and escape the pressures and stresses of the day. We found ourselves at a popular restaurant based on a friend's recommendation. We were attracted to the restaurant by the well-designed building, well-groomed gardens, and clean, well-lit parking lot. I noticed the cleanliness of the sidewalk entryway and front door glass. We were concerned about the number of people in the lobby and expected a seating delay. A friendly host welcomed us as we entered the lobby. She looked happy we were there and as if she had been expecting us. I immediately felt an exceptional warmth from her friendliness and realized we were in a very special place. We were immediately seated comfortably at a table and then were told about the specials of the day. We were astonished by the friendliness of the staff. Everyone I saw was cheerful, made direct eye contact, and exhibited an interest in our enjoyment. I did not see a staff member in personal conversation; they were all hustling about and appeared to have a passion for serving Guests as fast as possible. The dining room floors and the restrooms were spotlessly clean. Tables were cleared quickly after guests left, and we never saw a table left unattended with dirty dishes. I was surprised at how new the place looked. All the counters, station booths, and tables were clean, and all surfaces were in good repair. The dining room was orderly, with everything in its place. There was no indication that anyone had previously eaten at our table. The atmosphere was fun and festive. It was attractive and comfortable, with good air circulation. The décor and lighting created a festive mood with interesting artifacts reminiscent of "Old World" food processes. The glass and brass fixtures were brightly polished.

We were welcomed at the table by a friendly manager and, moments later, a friendly server in a spotlessly clean uniform. She introduced herself by name. Her name was Megan. She seemed happy to be helping us. Megan took our order efficiently, suggested items to go with our meals, and then made sure she understood precisely what each of us wanted. She knew all about the menu and helped with our questions. Megan served our beverages immediately, and our salad came soon after, even thought she was busy serving other tables. Another friendly server served our order. We were taken by surprise at how quickly our order had been prepared. Everyone's food looked delightful, and we all raved about how delicious they tasted. It was prepared exactly as we ordered. Our service was uninterrupted and flowed smoothly throughout the meal. The manager asked about drink refills, and another server brought them. Our service needs were taken care of without our asking. Our server or the manager was there when needed but never interrupted or dominated our attention. We didn't have to ask for anything and never experienced even the slightest wait. A staff member quietly removed dishes from our table as soon as they were emptied. Megan was so descriptive about the desserts we just had to order them. We Enjoyed them immensely.

The service of tables around us seemed to be orchestrated by the manager throughout our meal. He was involved in our service from his initial welcome and friendly conversation to assisting with our service as needed. Everyone seemed to be working smoothly together as a team to serve us. They were focused on serving Guests and appeared to be exceptionally well trained and professional with their work. I noticed the manager personally helping other parties and directing staff members, ensuring excellent *and fast service for all. Megan brought our check before we finished our desserts. We paid our check and left a generous tip. As we prepared to go, the manager expressed a sincere thank you. On the way out, two other staff members said thank you. I felt refreshed and found myself thinking, **hat was a very Enjoyable experience.** I feel like coming back next week and bringing friends."*

MAKING DECISIONS FOR CHANGE AND IMPROVEMENT

Making decisions for change and improvement is not always easy. Some decisions are no-brainers, while others take time and involve many considerations. You must weigh the ultimate benefits to your guests, your staff, and your restaurant's profits. What will the costs be? How long will it take to implement? There are seldom clear answers regarding the benefits to the guests. How will it affect their dining experience? How will they respond?

All decisions that affect guests and your restaurant's image are difficult to judge at best. These decisions must be made with your ultimate goals and the image of your restaurant in mind. Ensure that any changes will strengthen your restaurant's image. It takes faith to make these decisions, knowing that the actual results and benefits may never be evident to you.

"The Brick Oven Dining Experience Is About to Begin, The Curtain Is Going Up."

"At one time, we made this 'announcement' over the restaurant's speaker system to our staff just before opening the doors for our Guests. A full-service restaurant experience is like a stage performance. There are actors, stage managers, directors, scripts, costumes, staging, props, concessions and an audience. When we treated our restaurant's dining room like a stage performance, we better caught the essence of what we were really doing. We were entertaining our Guests. We were like a miniature Disneyland experience, giving extraordinary attention to details. We could be a unique world of our own. We could distract people from the cares of the world. They can escape their trials and problems for an hour. Unlike the outside world, we tried to provide a space where there were no problems, no waiting, no mistakes, no hassles, no chaos, no pressures, no disagreements, no bad news. It is a "Totally Enjoyable Experience."

This exercise taught our staff that working in a restaurant was indeed a performance.

If you control everything that guest senses in, around, and about your restaurant, you influence what they see, smell, taste, hear, and feel. By doing so, you can shape their future behavior. If everything they sense and feel is positive, they will have no choice but to return to your restaurant for future dining experiences.

Create a vision and standards of how you envision your restaurant operating for the benefit of your guests and staff members.

Guests are aware of your staff members' positive work attitudes.

Staff members are smiling, having fun at work, and exhibiting a cooperative attitude between staff and management.

Working at your restaurant is challenging for staff members as they learn essential skills for their future careers.

Staff member parties and activities are provided periodically to say thank you and recognize their achievements as a team (e.g., new productivity or sales records).

Awards such as "Associate of the Month," "Associate of the Year," and "Manager of the Year" are presented to outstanding associates and managers.

Staff members are provided opportunities to associate outside of work to team-build without work pressures. Have summer, holiday, or other parties, social events, or community service projects together as a team.

Working conditions are well thought out, such as having a brightly lit kitchen for clear food production and facilities laid out to facilitate staff efficiency.

The break rooms are accommodating and well-appointed for your staff members.

Staff members are treated with respect by management.

Managers and supervisors on duty are cross-trained in all positions they supervise and move spontaneously as needed from station to station to equalize the workload.

Managers are inspecting and overseeing the work of their subordinates, ensuring every product is prepared correctly and served immediately.

Staff members on duty look happy and proficient, wearing their professional uniforms.

Staff members are highly motivated and proud to be serving food that guests love.

Staff members are made to feel appreciated for their good work by management.

During slow business periods, staff members are busy stocking up on food and supplies, preparing for busy periods.

Staff members show respect for each other and cheerfully assist each other as a team.

Staff members are willing to stay late or come early depending on the restaurant's needs.

Staff members respond to management's directions in a cooperative manner.

Staff members are energetic and eager to do their work correctly.

Trainee staff members are identifiable to guests and are receiving the help they need to become fully trained by management and more experienced staff members.

Kitchen cooks and dining room servers cooperate so the guest receives fast, friendly service and delicious food that looks delightful.

DEVELOP YOUR RESTAURANT'S STANDARDS AND IMAGE

Identify your primary prospective guests. What group of people are you primarily trying to attract and serve? This is crucial when deciding what kind of restaurant you want to be. Consider the following questions to narrow down your target audience:

What type of food do they want?

What atmosphere do they prefer?

What sounds are pleasant to them?

Are you aiming for a casual or formal setting?

Will your restaurant be full-service, self-service, or fast-casual?

What is your primary customer's price sensitivity? Should your prices be low, medium, or high?

Does your customer want breakfast, lunch, or dinner?

Are your guests mainly businesspeople, families, singles, or a mix?

Are they students with limited time and budget?

Where do they live or work, and how far are they from your restaurant?

Is your primary customer a mother with a large family who decides where to dine?

Once you determine your primary customer, you'll be better positioned to shape your restaurant's image to attract them consistently. Remember, you can't please everyone and shouldn't try. By narrowing your focus, you can present a strong, cohesive image to your prime guests. Each visit to your restaurant will either enhance or diminish a guest's image of your establishment.

Your restaurant's image must exude quality, encompassing friendliness, service, cleanliness, delicious food, and ambiance. It must be consistent and reliable with every visit.

Quality can be defined as a product or service produced precisely as designed and intended every single time. For instance, both a Cadillac and a Volkswagen can be quality products if they meet their design specifications consistently. The cost is irrelevant.

Design products and services that are desirable to your intended guests. The more significant challenge is producing them consistently each time. Handling variable food products, maintaining food characteristics during storage and holding, and ensuring consistent preparation by staff are all part of this challenge.

"A mental image exists in an individual's mind, as something one remembers or imagines. It is what people think of anything, including a restaurant. The subject of an image need not be real; it may be an abstract concept, such as a graph, function, or 'imaginary' entity."

–Wikipedia

DETERMINE YOUR RESTAURANT'S VISION

A vision establishes the image (brand) you aim to create in the minds of your prospective guests. This vision shapes how people perceive your restaurant and significantly influences your success. A mental picture of a restaurant is a shared conception held by a community, symbolizing its essential attitude and orientation. Each person can have a slightly different image of a restaurant based on their individual experiences.

A disorderly or disorganized restaurant facility can seriously tarnish your restaurant's community image. The image is the perception people have about your restaurant, significantly affecting its success. What others think and feel about your restaurant prompts them to patronize it. Your restaurant's image encompasses what it offers in terms of aesthetics, flavors, and service experiences.

Your personal image has many elements: the way you dress and groom, your hairstyle, the colors you wear, how you talk and act, and how you relate to others. The car you drive, your family, and your friends also contribute. The same principles apply to a restaurant. What does your restaurant look and feel like? You need to manage your restaurant's image just as you manage your personal image. If you haven't thought about your image and how you present yourself to others, it's crucial to start now, as it affects your success.

"If you carry about with you a disturbing or disagreeable mental defect, it needs not be named and known to work its poison upon your affairs. Its corrosive influence will eat into all your efforts, and disfigure your happiness and prosperity, as powerful acid eats

into and disfigures the finest steel. On the other hand, if you carry about an assuring and harmonious mental excellence, it needs not that those about you understand it to be influenced by it to be influenced by it. They will be drawn towards you in goodwill, often without knowing why, and that good quality will be the most powerful support in your affairs, bringing you friends and opportunities, and greatly aiding in the success of all your enterprises. It will even right your minor incapacitates covering a multitude of faults."

–James Allen, *The Eight Pillars of Prosperity.*

CONSIDERATIONS FOR YOUR RESTAURANT'S IMAGE

When crafting your restaurant's image, you need to consider every aspect of your facilities, including carefully:

Your restaurant's logo

Exterior design and interior décor

Seating arrangements

Signage, Landscaping & Lighting

Walkways, receiving-door porch, and trash dumpster area. Your staff's appearance, behavior, service style, and techniques are crucial components of your image. Additionally, consider the presentation and style of your menu, your food product mix, and how food is served. Elements such as advertising style, the font used in promotional materials, service, and glassware presentation also contribute to your restaurant's overall image. Essentially, your image encompasses everything the public sees, experiences, or hears about your restaurant, including your personal image and that of your staff.

Key factors that influence your restaurant's success include location visibility, neighborhood, ease of access, and adequate parking.

Cleanliness and sanitation are vital aspects of a restaurant's image. Here are ways to manage this critical factor:

Ensure all windows, mirrors, cabinets, and fixtures are clean and free of soil and fingerprints. A facility's cleanliness should be apparent as either bright and crisp or dim and indistinct.

Pay special attention to restroom fixtures, doorknobs, and condiment shakers, as these are critical to guests' perceptions of cleanliness.

While caution signs placed over floor spills are necessary for safety, they can detract from a restaurant's image if left in view too long or if they become dirty. Avoid anything that mars the visual appeal of your restaurant, as these factors collectively shape the public's perception.

Potential guests choose which restaurant to patronize based on their image of each option. Your goal should be to create the most favorable image in the minds of potential guests compared to competing restaurants.

Whenever someone decides to dine out, the images of various restaurant options compete in their mind. The winner is the restaurant with the strongest positive image, gaining the customer's patronage. As a restaurant operator, strive to maintain a favorable image so your restaurant is always considered a top option. Your restaurant's image constantly competes with others of the same type within your market area. Understanding how you stack up against competitors is crucial, as the strongest image ultimately influences where patrons choose to dine.

Strengthening Your Restaurant's Image

To make your restaurant's image (brand) strong, you must ensure that all components are consistent and unified. A strong brand is competitive because all elements of your restaurant's image are well-matched and complementary. When elements fit together harmoniously, they strengthen the overall theme of your restaurant. For example, if your restaurant is full-service with nice booths, the glassware should be glass rather than plastic or paper. Cloth napkins suggest a step above paper, hinting at a higher level of service.

A professional graphics artist can help match your intended image with the correct font style for your menu, ads, and signage. Decorators, architects, builders, chefs, designers, stylists, and artists all contribute to communicating your vision to your guests. Ultimately, you must judge whether your graphics designer and decorator have suggested the proper image for your establishment. Implementing a visually satisfying facility that aligns with and strengthens your brand is essential.

Your chef's menu recipes must align with your restaurant's image. They should be logical and consistent with your restaurant's name and style. For instance, serving Asian food in a Western-style BBQ restaurant would be inconsistent. The food must be delicious and align with all other elements of your vision.

Your restaurant's image is composed of multiple events that guests and potential guests experience. These events include:

The appearance of the building and parking lot

The front door and entryway

Interactions with their greeter and their server

Seating and service process from order-taking to serving

The interval between ordering and receiving food

The appearance and flavor of the food and beverages

The cleanliness and ambiance of the restroom

Observing other guests

Each event must be attractive, comfortable, relaxing, delicious, delightful, and satisfying. Every positive and pleasing event strengthens guests' images of your restaurant. The stronger their positive image, the more likely they are to return, even in the face of competition.

Avoid exposing guests to anything unattractive, uncomfortable, stressful, distasteful, unpleasant, or unenjoyable. Such negatives detract from your restaurant's positive image. *When you find something about your restaurant that distracts from your guest's enjoyment, fix it immediately.*

Convenience also plays a significant role in dining decisions. The proximity of your location to guests' homes or workplaces, ease of access from roads and freeways, convenient parking, and safe walkways and entrances all contribute to your restaurant's appeal.

Consistency is key. Delivering consistently pleasant food, service, facilities, and décor strengthens your image. A strong, unique image sets your restaurant apart from the competition. The consistency of this sensory package determines your sales volume and guest counts. Positive, enjoyable experiences enhance your restaurant's image, while negative experiences damage it.

Providing continually improving experiences for your guests can be challenging. Taking guest experiences seriously may be stressful, but it is essential. Better system development and staff management are crucial. A negative image can lead guests to stop patronizing your restaurant, often without consciously knowing why.

The restaurant business is all about creating an enjoyable experience for guests. It involves food recipes, facility design and construction, value for money, and service. Each of these factors can be broken down further:

Facilities: Design, upkeep, cleanliness, sanitation, décor quality, and room temperature.

Value: Selection of pricing options, portion size, and overall value received by guests.

Service: Staff appearance, service techniques, promptness, manners, friendliness, and attitudes toward guests.

Creating these factors in a synchronized, consistent, and pleasant way is the challenge of operating a successful restaurant. These elements, both consciously and unconsciously, are evident to most guests.

Kevin R. Miller, in his book *Customers Only Want Two Things,* explains: *"Leave Me Feeling Great about the Experience. Ultimately, loyalty is an emotional feeling won in the hearts and then minds of others. When someone leaves feeling great about the service experience, it plants in their heart a nearly unforgettable emotion that lingers far into the future. And this is where many businesses, including schools break down. They are content with solving the customer's problems and meeting customer's needs. Customers leave satisfied but not loyal. And they are easily wooed away by the competition.*

*Here we add the second part of the leave me feeling great component: **Be uniquely nice to me.** Unique means something special, something singular, that leaves the customer feeling like they were more than a number or transaction, something that bonds them."*

THIRD KEY TO $UCCESS
SYSTEMATIZE YOUR RESTAURANT OPERATIONS

Install Systems, Schedules, and Training to Ensure the Restaurant's Enjoyment Standards for Staff and Management Job Satisfaction are Always Met.

ORGANIZING YOUR RESTAURANT

You must invest the time and effort necessary to develop a comprehensive and detailed plan for your restaurant's concept and brand. Every detail must be identified and determined. You need to carefully plan, outline, and document your operational systems, procedures, and methods.

It's essential to remain fluid and flexible with your concept, ready to make subtle or significant changes as you discover the deeper preferences and newly developed needs and wants of your primary guests. Identifying who your primary guests are and understanding who you will cater to is crucial.

The Importance of Planning in Business

In any business, time spent planning is the most valuable time. Developing themes and concepts, procedures, methods, operating systems, values, recipes, and standards is critical. **Plan your work, then work your plan.** Shooting from the hip is a terrible business practice. *Letting staff members or management decide how and what is done is a recipe for failure.*

Your decisions and systems must align with and be performed with your guests' wants and needs in mind. Understand the difference between doing work excellently, with precision and accuracy, and merely going through the motions.

Grasp the distinction between a laborer, an artisan, and an artist. Appreciate the artistic nature of a restaurant, which is a coordinated performance of facilities, food, and service. Strive to become an artist in the restaurant business by mastering the details of the industry and working with your heart.

"He who works with his hands is a laborer; He who works with his hands and his head is an artisan; He who works with his hands and his head, and his heart is an artist."

–T.V. Smith, American philosopher and politician

You Must Win the Battles to Win the War

Sun Tzu was a Chinese general, military strategist, and philosopher who lived in ancient China. Sun Tzu is traditionally credited as the author of *The Art of War,* a widely influential work of military strategy that has affected both Western and Eastern philosophy. His principles of war can be applied to any project or endeavor, including a restaurant.

Foretelling Triumph

"Those who triumph, compute at their headquarters a great number of factors prior to a challenge.

Those who are defeated compute at their headquarters a small number of factors prior to a challenge.

Much computation brings triumph.

Little computation brings defeat.

How much more so with no computation at all!

By observing only this, I can see triumph or defeat."

Consider Writing a Promise Statement

A "Promise Statement" Example:

"We guarantee a thoroughly enjoyable experience for every guest. We pride ourselves on providing delicious food, fast, friendly service, a sparkling clean restaurant, and a festive atmosphere. No one should leave our restaurant unhappy. If any aspect of your food or service falls below excellent, please report it directly to the manager on duty. Your satisfaction is our top priority, and we deeply appreciate your feedback."

Kitchen Staff's Promise

"We promise to prepare every dish precisely according to recipe and deliver it to the dining room and to-go counter in less than __ minutes."

Dining Room Staff's Promise

"We promise that guests will never wait to be seated unless every table is occupied. We commit to taking and clarifying every guest's order within __ minutes of seating and entering it into the computer immediately and accurately. We pledge to serve all dishes

to guests within __ minutes of preparation and maintain attentiveness to overall dining room service."

Consider Writing a Mission Statement

Present your mission to your staff members so they are clear on what you are trying to accomplish. Clearly state your restaurant's mission statement. Manage your staff to meet your guests' expectations. As an operator, you must empathize with your guests. Many staff members may lack successful restaurant work experience, awareness of guest experience requirements, and guest empathy.

Example Mission Statement:

"To create an enjoyable stop along the way for nourishment and refreshment, encouraging guests to return often because they feel welcome and enjoy food that looks delightful and tastes delicious, served promptly in a clean, festive atmosphere."

A Passion for Your Restaurant's Mission

Your passions might include:

Creating enjoyment for guests

Creating financial and professional opportunities for the restaurant and your staff

Improving your community

Having fun

When you are driven and passionate, your work reflects the desires of your heart, allowing you to perform with exhilaration and without regret. *You must create a work environment that is relentless in pursuing excellence.*

Position Mission Statements:

Dining Room Manager's Mission: "To encourage guests to return often by hiring, training, and coaching staff members in the preparation and service of food and beverages in a clean, festive atmosphere, according to operational systems."

Kitchen Manager's Mission: "To encourage guests to return often by hiring, training, and coaching staff members in food preparation, receiving, and storage of materials in a clean, sanitary kitchen, according to operational recipes and systems."

Consider Writing a Purpose Statement

Purpose Statement Example:

"Our restaurant's purpose is not just to make a sale today; it is to sell guests on coming back tomorrow."

Every day, you and your restaurant staff should be "working on tomorrow." The majority of your guests today will be previous guests unless your business is located in a transient area like a freeway or a point of interest for vacationers. In that case, your efforts should focus primarily on marketing to them via location, signage, or media they will likely access.

You prepare for next month by creating demand in the minds of guests today by keeping 100% of your promises to them. Remember, people who come to your restaurant are not yours, and you do not own them. Nor can you be sure they will return. Most of the sales you make today result from your work yesterday. Your job is to make the experience so valuable that it attracts your guests back tomorrow.

Occasionally, I would take a manager into our dining room and ask who the people dining were. When they said, "they are our guests," I would explain that they are really "prospective guests" for tomorrow's business. They have demonstrated interest in our restaurant. Our job is to sell them on coming back tomorrow. We cannot afford to give them reasons not to return through mediocre service, food, cleanliness, or facility conditions. Every day is your chance to sell guests on your excellent service, delicious food, clean, sanitary, and well-appointed facilities.

You can control what people see, hear, smell, feel, and taste while they are in and around your restaurant. To consistently bring guests back, you must provide these four conditions:

Clean, sanitary conditions

Fast, friendly, professional staff members

Food that looks delightful and tastes delicious

A pleasant environment

Consider Writing a Vision Statement

Vision Statement Example:

"We are a growing restaurant company known to be the best, where guests feel welcome and perceive us as providing delicious food, fast, friendly service in a clean, festive atmosphere."

Dining at your restaurant should be a fun experience with generous portions of fresh, flavorful foods that look delightful and taste delicious. Your restaurant should be known throughout your market area for high-quality food, fast-friendly service, and a festive atmosphere. Your facilities should always be spotlessly clean. Your menu prices should be reasonable and match the value you provide guests.

Successful marketing means guests realize your restaurant is superior to all competition. They must recognize a significant difference between you and other available choices and prefer yours over others. Great guest service is defined as "a positive, reassuring, and pleasant encounter with a responsive, responsible person." All staff members, including managers and owners, work for the guests. Without the guests, there would be no restaurant.

Ronald Reagan's quote:

"To grasp and hold a vision, that is the very essence of successful leadership-not only on the movie set where I learned it, but everywhere."

THE POWER OF PASSION IN YOUR RESTAURANT

Passion is a personal intensity, the underlying force that fuels your strongest emotions. You can recognize it by what it does: passion fills you with energy and excitement. It gets you up in the morning and keeps you awake at night. When you experience passion, you lose track of time and become absorbed in the task at hand. It uplifts and inspires you, heightens your performance, and enables you to achieve things you may never have dreamed possible.

A restaurant filled with passion is a different kind of place. You sense something unique the moment you walk in the door; something is inviting and engaging about the atmosphere. It is filled with an air of enthusiasm, energy, and excitement. The staff is friendly, the environment is comfortable, and the overall experience is pleasant. Staff members seem genuinely interested in guests and eager to help.

Passion creates a noticeable energy within an organization, transforming the very nature of its activities. It infuses the organization with a quality and vitality that otherwise would not be present. Passion transforms the ordinary into the extraordinary. It provides direction and focus, creates energy, and fosters creativity. Passion heightens performances and inspires action, attracting both staff members and guests. Passion builds loyalty and unites an organization, providing the competitive edge that stands head and shoulders above mere enthusiasm.

The foundation of a successful company is a sincere trust and belief in people. Your goal should be to hire individuals who are passionate about improvements and share your enthusiasm for creating enjoyment for guests. When staff members are passionate about their work, they should be trusted, believed in, and made integral to the company's progress. They must be rewarded for taking the initiative to improve systems. Conversely, anyone who is not passionate about your restaurant's mission has no business being involved with it.

Walt Disney's answer to the question:

"What do we need to do to better succeed with our cartoons?

He responded,

"Make better drawings." - Details, Details, Details.

ADOPT STRONG COMPANY VALUES

Strong company values are necessary for any business to succeed. These values are crucial for success, determining how you treat each other and conducting your business. Teach your people these values and help them adopt them.

Cleanliness and Orderliness: Ensure the cleanliness and orderliness of your offices, kitchens, walk-in refrigerators, drawers, files, shelves, storage facilities, equipment, customer service areas, closets, and restrooms. Keep your restaurant and grounds free from clutter, litter, stains, smudges, dust, and dirt.

Punctuality and Timeliness: Arrive on time for work, breaks, meals, and meetings. Reply to letters and phone calls, pay bills, and make payroll on time.

Speed of Operations: Measure the speed and timeliness of service delivery, ensuring actions occur as quickly as possible.

Attention to Detail: Pay special attention to details that are obvious to your guests but may only be noticed by you upon careful inspection of your restaurant's operations.

Honesty and Integrity: Foster an environment where staff members enjoy working for a company that promotes good work ethics.

Respect and Trust: Promote an environment of respect and trust. Trusting relationships are free from fear, suspicion, and intimidation. Keep the promises and commitments you make.

Positive Attitude: No factor has a greater influence on your success than attitude. Your personal feelings about your job are instantly recognizable to others.

Safety: Maintain safety in production and service areas vehicles, for staff members and guests.

Fairness: Maintain high standards without political influences or favoritism. Provide opportunities for staff members' advancement and compensation based on job proficiency and merit.

Customer Delight and Enjoyment: The positive emotional response and joy that customers feel from interactions with your staff, management, and products and services determine your success.

Decisiveness: Being decisive in solving problems, planning, executing plans, and committing to decisions once made is critical to your success.

Respect for the Individual: Show respect for individuals when establishing rules and policies, designing systems, making decisions, and executing instructions, considering people's safety, feelings, and opinions.

Service to Society: Demonstrate commitment to your community welfare, environmental protection, and developing products and services that meet real physical, social, or psychological needs.

Harmony: Foster an overall atmosphere and interaction among people, departments, systems, activities, rules, and policies within the company and between these elements and the external environment, guests, vendors, community laws, and so on.

Dependability and Consistency: Always do what you say you will do when operating your systems. Ensure facilities, products, and services are consistently performed and presented the same way.

Friendliness: People do business where they feel welcome and appreciated. Being friendly towards each other and guests is the cornerstone of your success.

Creativity: Find new ways to serve guests better.

Quality: Ensure products and services are produced precisely as designed and according to the customer's preferences and expectations, including presentation, choice, value for money, suitability, shelf life, courtesy, friendliness, etc.

Clean & Sanitary Environment: Keep your restaurant spotlessly clean and free from litter.

Economy: Recycle materials and avoid unnecessary waste of food, supplies, utilities, and labor.

"A value statement isn't essential to the running of a company, but companies need to have a clear idea of who they are. And they want the public and their employees to understand that identity. Simply put, a value statement is a declaration that

announces a company's top priorities and core beliefs, both to guide their employees' actions and to connect with consumers."

–Steffani Cameron - Bizfluent article October 26, 2018

Value Statement Example:

The purpose of your values is to explain to your staff members how to behave and what to expect while working at your restaurant to achieve personal and company growth.

"We believe in being honest and ethical in all our dealings with each other and our guests visiting the restaurant. We are willing to take risks and accept failures in the pursuit of excellence. We recognize the needs and talents of our people and work to foster open communication. We provide fair compensation based on productivity and results. We fulfill our potential by cooperating in developing new and improved methods and procedures, which assure progress and growth. We encourage suggestions, creative thoughts, and ideas to improve our systems.

We pledge to our staff members to hire the best-qualified personnel and provide them with effective training. We guarantee to provide staff members with the most adequate benefits, proper motivation, and fair treatment. We hire individuals capable of constant change because we are continually seeking more productive methods to perform our work. Guests appreciate progressive change and enjoy frequenting establishments that stay in tune with the times. Change is necessary for growth.

When a policy is revised, the company will take steps to communicate changes to all relevant persons, including management, supervisory personnel, and other staff members, on a need-to-know basis."

SYSTEMATIZE YOUR RESTAURANT

Systems are Solutions

Aim to please the most demanding guests by developing unique systems designed to ensure their enjoyment.

Systems are developed to achieve consistent results that create guest enjoyment and produce a profit. If a process is not documented, it will never be executed with any degree of consistency; it will eventually evolve, change, or cease. It is impossible to work in unity and provide consistent results without a written plan for everyone to follow. Systems are based on measurable results.

My motivation for systemization began around 1990. Zions Bank invited Michael Gerber to Salt Lake City for a one-day seminar for its clients. I attended the meetings and met Michael. I was impressed with his message about the advantages of systematizing a business so it could be operated more effectively, expanded if desired, and sold more easily. I later became a client of Michael's company. His organization helped me systematize my restaurant. Later, I appeared with Michael in a satellite national broadcast for the U.S. Chamber of Commerce in Washington, D.C., where I shared how systemization revolutionized the operation of my business.

Every System Requires Inspection, Follow-Up, and Oversight to Thrive

Written systems allow you to plan your work and work your plan. They are developed to create guest enjoyment consistently. Valid systems are written and based on measurable results rather than opinions. Properly performed systems achieve consistent, reliable results that help ensure the success of any business. Every system can and must be performed correctly each time. Your people must execute systems 100%. We intend to perform ordinary work extraordinarily well. "Most of the time" and "usually" are not good enough to succeed. Your systems should be fair, reasonable, and humane. They become "The Way We Do It Here."

Managing Isn't About Doing Things - It's About Getting Things Done

Managing is about knowing what needs to be done and finding a way to get it done without doing it yourself. The job of managing is different from the job of your subordinates. By doing their work, you may be unable to do yours. While there are times when a manager must be a worker, these times should be kept to a minimum. Managers should watch the work of subordinates just as their managers watch theirs. Monitoring the systems you have installed is crucial to keeping them operating correctly and accurately.

Managers are often promoted from staff member positions. They are usually very successful and comfortable doing that work. However, being paid as a manager while doing the work of staff members will lead to failure. An effective manager uses their previous experience as a staff member to relate to their subordinates' work but minimizes doing it themselves. Doing subordinates' work distracts the manager from their task of observing the work process and offering compliments or assistance only when needed.

Systemization: Systems Dependent, Not People Dependent

The basic view of systemization is that your business is systems-dependent, not people-dependent. While this is true, it's important to note that even the most sophisticated systems require qualified, committed people to use and improve them.

Systems are not designed to wring humanity out of your company. Rather, they free your staff from daily concerns such as, "How do we wait at a table? How do we answer telephones? How do we stock our salad bar? How is this entrée prepared?" With systems in place, everyone can focus on "How can we do it better?" The general idea of systemization is to move your organization closer to being a precision operation in all aspects of its functioning. Your restaurant becomes more dependable and consistent each day. Every system eliminates some risk in operating the restaurant. Every system is important for a restaurant to succeed.

Develop Operating Manuals

No operating manual can be self-enforcing. No matter how intelligent and clearly written, it will become a dust catcher unless management continually reinforces its value. It must become the official, reliable, authoritative source of information about your restaurant, its products, and the "rules of your game." It can also explain the logic behind your systems.

Operating manuals can contain:

Staff Member Handbook, Compensation and Benefits Handbook, and Dress Code

Your restaurant's strategic objective, history, and organization chart

Position-specific agreements and lists of operating procedures

Checklists; descriptions of your products, services, and recipes; forms and scripts

Policies, flow charts, mission statement, values, and vision

"System is that principle of order by which confusion is rendered impossible. In the natural and universal order everything is in its place, so that the vast universes runs more perfectly than the most perfect machine. Disorder in space would mean the destruction of the universe; and disorder in a man's affairs destroys his work and his prosperity. All complex organizations are built up by systems. No business society can develop into large dimension apart from systems and this principle is preeminently the instrument of the merchant, the businessman, and the organizer of institutions."

–James Allen, *The Eight Pillars of Prosperity* (p. 45).

An excerpt from Michael E. Gerber's article, author of *The E-Myth Revisited*, published in Inc. magazine, titled "Why Do It All Yourself? Documenting Your Success."

"Ever since we launched Radical U earlier this year, people have been asking me why? Simple. Over the decades of working with small businesses, it's become obvious to me that the thing that separates successful companies from failing ones is the presence of a process to how that company is run. Think about it - do you train employees 'on the job' or do you have manuals to handle that? If you're doing on the job training, how many times do new employees know exactly what to do in every situation? None. How about who to ask for answers? Yes, none again.

So why do so many companies fail to simply create a documentable process for something as important can costly as hiring and training?

So, I started Radical U to teach people the process to become successful entrepreneurs. An operational manual for how to start, grow, run, and eventually sell their own successful small business.

Just like you need to teach your new employees the process to becoming successful employees with your own operational manual for how they can learn the job and the various responsibilities that come with employment in your business.

Documenting either one of these ideas - Radical U for me and your business for you - stem from the same basic thought - no one can know it all and with a standard resource, it becomes less about the skill level and more about the engagement level.

Think of a McDonald's French fry. Hot, fresh, crispy, perfectly salted. Now, you can teach someone how to do that by hand, or you can document that fries are cooked for a certain amount of time in grease of a certain temperature, salted with a certain number of shakes from a certain shaker, and thrown away if they are a certain number of minutes old. One system needs a chef, the other needs a willing employee. Which is easier to find?

So, if you haven't committed to documenting every process in your business as a training tool, why? There are huge benefits to it - think about it.

Operational manuals help you in the hiring process. You are able to get even the greenest new hire a wealth of basic information instantly. It's an overview of everything they can expect from the job and your company.

Training is made easier, since you can easily document every standard, not just the ones your team remembers to teach a new employee. Teaching new people doesn't have to be people-dependent, it can now be systems-dependent. You can build the entire training process around the operations manual and vice-versa.

You no longer must act as the repository for every standard, every action, and everything the business needs to do. That means that "regular" people can play important roles with far less skills than you once needed. Think how simple you could make the process of invoicing? Payroll? Shipping? Sales? All without you having to be the one doing it.

Your entire business is documented. Simply put, when someone walks in the door and wants to buy your company, you can point to the operations manuals and tell them, "Here's how we do it here." Even better? That documentation validates your system works leading to two positive outcomes - the buyer knows it works and you, as the seller, won't undervalue how well it works."

EVERY FRUSTRATION IS THE RESULT OF THE LACK OF A SYSTEM

85% of your problems will occur in processes or systems, and only 15% are due to people. A system is simply the way you do something repeatedly. Unfortunately, too few people realize they are using a system and make the mistake of doing what doesn't work time and time again, expecting their frustrations to disappear.

You need to recognize that the way you do something is a system, and the only way to improve the outcome is to improve the system. Finding the right system will eliminate any frustration.

Your Restaurant Reflects Yourself

The way a restaurant operates and conducts itself is a direct reflection of the operator. If the management is disorganized, lacks vision, and is sloppy, the unit will also be disorganized, lack vision, and perform sloppily. Conversely, if the managers are focused, organized, and conduct themselves with forethought, the unit will reflect these characteristics.

Strategic Work

Reaching your objectives requires strategic work. This means working on, not in, your restaurant. You must be involved in organizing, planning, developing, and operating your restaurant to move continuously toward your goals. You can't simply sell products or services, deliver them, handle the money, hire and fire people, etc. You must continually analyze how all that is done and develop systems to produce the predictable results you and your guests want.

Keep it Simple

Systems should be as simple as possible—a system that is complicated to the point where people can't understand or use it defeats the purpose of having a system. Remember this rule: keep it short and simple. Even the most complicated things can be systematized. Complexity can always be broken down into simple, manageable elements. In this way, even the most complex systems break down into a connected set of elementary subsystems.

Understanding Frustration

Frustration is an undesirable pattern of events over which you feel you have little or no control. Frustration happens when someone is doing the wrong thing, and your efforts to fix it don't work. It is an unwanted pattern of events. Frustration has an emotional charge to it—exasperation, blame, confusion, even anger.

We are talking about frustrations experienced by people who are interested in the long-term success of the company and are worried about how guests are served, how staff members are managed, or the profitability of the company.

Systems Reduce People's Problems

Systems help reduce people's problems and screen out inaccurate perceptions. Establishing a sound system can eliminate most frustrations. The heart of developing profitable systems lies in understanding the basic conditions that are causing the frustration. The key to removing frustration is to create effective profitability systems that cure underlying problems.

Perceiving Frustrations

There are three ways people perceive frustrations:

I am the problem.

Someone or something else is the cause.

We lack an effective profitability system.

Numbers 1 and 2 are misdirected. The actual cause of business frustrations is always the lack of an effective system. All business frustrations are system-directed. That's not to say that people are never the problem—sometimes they are. But that, too is made clear by creating a profitability system. If people are unwilling or unable to perform a profitability system, it becomes clear in an objective, dispassionate way and without blame.

Profitability Systems Free People

Profitability systems free people: they don't restrict them. They free staff members from laboring over the most routine and repetitive elements of work, allowing them to concentrate on what's most unique in the situation. They can focus on their growth and development because they are awake and aware at times.

> *"Some people regard discipline as a chore. For me, it is a kind of order that sets me free to fly."*
>
> –Julie Andrews, actress

Focus on Guests

Your profitability systems should focus on guests. Growing companies are focused on customer satisfaction. Aim to exceed guests' enjoyment expectations. Your systems will be developed to solve problems and will become the way your restaurant does business. Every opportunity (problem) requires a profitability system (plan) to achieve a result. Your staff then follows that plan exactly each and every time.

Meeting guests' needs essentially means providing them with products and services that fully meet or exceed their requirements for enjoyment. First, it is crucial to define those needs and expectations. Profitability systems management is a method aimed at exceeding guests' needs for enjoyment at the lowest cost.

Generally, a result would be to create enjoyment for guests or contribute toward the profitability of your restaurant. A correctly stated result or objective will allow interested parties to come up with other actions or steps that may be simpler or more effective in reaching the result or objective of the system.

Every system will have steps or actions to take to accomplish the result or objective of the system. Every operating system might include standards or conditions.

> *"Get the facts, or the facts will get you. And when you get 'em, get 'em right, or they will get you wrong."*
>
> –Thomas Fuller, English clergyman

Manage Profitability Systems by Facts

Management by fact is based on the theory that decisions are founded on objective, relevant, and quantifiable data rather than on opinions or impressions. Management, in fact, means improving your work processes using statistical methods based on measurements.

Changing profitability systems requires objectivity and unity. Effective companies create a culture that accepts change. Informed change, based on objectivity, is a necessary way of life in a growing company. When a profitability system is changed, staff members must be retrained.

Profitability systems respect people. To provide guests with enjoyable products and services, we rely on the commitment of staff members. Showing respect for staff members means providing them with complete training, inviting their comments and suggestions, taking their opinions into account, implementing the factual solutions they propose, and recognizing their efforts.

Thus, you should:

Acknowledge that people using or supervising systems are best suited for improving them.

Utilize staff member know-how to identify work necessary to achieve improvement targets.

Provide staff members with the necessary tools and involve them in decision-making processes.

Promote participatory management and the development of staff members.

Profitability systems require management support. Let systems determine the work. Management must know and support every policy, system, and standard. Managers must stand on their own authority and never use a superior's name, such as "Sam wants you to do this" or "Mr. Smith saw you do that." Using someone's name while supervising weakens a manager's position and diminishes subordinates' respect.

We see a restaurant's activities as a set of executed systems causing guests to perceive their experience as enjoyable. The role of management is to facilitate and coordinate the correct use of systems. Systems ensure that every event in a guest's experience is positive. Every event will have a system behind it. Systems minimize the need for work experience.

We don't need to hire people with expertise, previous experience, or common sense because they may bring poor habits and experiences that produce poor results. There is no mystery or magic in experience; it merely adds to the number of alternatives to solve a problem. Problems that need more experience are frequently solved by making someone do something for more years when the actual learning could be accomplished in a few days or weeks with systems that achieve desired results.

Committing Processes to Paper

Committing a process to paper is essential. When a system is not written, it is practically identical to having no system at all. Systems are created through experience, research, time, and money. Every step of each system is important and must be followed to develop guest enjoyment profitably. Verbal systems will not get the results you want; they are easily misunderstood or forgotten. They make a dependency on one person for instruction because they provide no reference to a system and become only temporary solutions.

Profitability Systems are the Key to the Future

Your company will exist only as long as it continues to do what is necessary for survival. Every year, companies that someone assumed would be here forever fail because they ceased to satisfy guests and be profitable. Your company is a lifeboat; if everyone doesn't do the right things, it will not survive. By following and improving systems, you ensure your future.

Profitability systems trade discretion for participation.

View staff members as a group of equally important individuals working together toward common goals and objectives. Everyone is invited to participate in improving systems by suggesting changes that would produce better results. Until a system is formally changed, everyone must follow the current system.

The profitability systems method of operating eliminates the discretion used to operate a personality-driven business. Systems quickly make experts out of inexperienced people who typically use experimentation to do the work. Profitability systems must be continuously improved.

Benefits of Profitability Systems

They are planned solutions to a result or process.

They eliminate knee-jerk, spontaneous reactions to problems.

They are a foundation for continuous improvement based on a commitment to quality.

They provide the ability to overcome inexperience and random experimentation with the work, thus reducing inconsistencies.

They represent a clear understanding of guest enjoyment requirements and specify the procedures and criteria to ensure conformity to those requirements.

They provide predictability, authority, responsibility, and accountability.

They provide consistent methods of operation and reduction of costs.

They are a documentation of the previous experience of many.

They provide consistent results that never fail.

Develop Written Profitability Systems

When your restaurant depends on the skills of individual people, you're not running it—they are. Profitability systems are developed in a manner that identifies and prevents the recurrence of frustrations and undesirable conditions relating to guest service or staff member management.

Whenever you experience a result that you do not like and want to avoid in the future, figure out a different course of action and plan out step by step what you will do or have others do. Repeat as necessary.

STEPS TO ADDRESS FRUSTRATIONS BY IMPROVING SYSTEMS

Step 1: State Your Frustration. Write a short statement in simple words as if you were speaking to someone. Avoid jumping to presumed solutions. You must be frustrated when guests are not delighted.

Step 2: Determine the Underlying Frustrating Conditions. Ask questions to get clarity on the cause of the frustration. Get to the real problem.

Step 3: Identify a System to Resolve the Frustration. Determine what result such a system needs to produce. Think systemically and overcome preconceived notions about people's dependency and blame. A system has a purpose—it delivers a result. An adequate system produces the exact result you intend, predictably, on time, on budget, every time. Reliability is the hallmark of an effective system. Divide the system into:

A result statement.

The process steps in the order necessary to achieve the result.

The standards under which the system is operated or the conditions under which it is performed.

The resulting statement is the intent of the system. If someone figures out a better way to achieve the result, you can modify the system accordingly.

Step 4: Design or Modify a System. Design or modify a system that produces the desired result, steps, and standards of performance to alleviate the frustration. This includes:

Designing operating forms, checklists, charts, and documents.

Writing scripts if needed.

Tracking the process and the necessary reports and checklists.

Designing the training program for staff members using the system.

Specifying the policies and rules required to enforce the process.

Determining a staff member notification and implementation plan.

Step 5: Implement the Profitability System and Train Staff Members. Implement the profitability system and immediately train staff members to operate it.

Standard for Operating System Development. All profitability systems should be quantified, tested, debugged, monitored, and modified as needed.

Monitoring and Refining the System. After implementing a system, monitor how successful it is in creating the desired results and refine the processes. Are there steps that are unclear to some staff members? Could there be simpler methods to achieve the desired results? Improving systems is an ongoing process as you move your restaurant closer to a precision operation.

Quantify Solutions Whenever Possible. Quantify a solution whenever possible to gain a clear understanding of the nature of the condition. Ask yourself questions like:

What percentage of the time does this frustrating condition occur?

How many times does this frustrating condition occur each day/week/month on average?

For example: "Our guests are not getting their orders when we promise" could be your frustration. The next question would be, "What percentage of orders are served late?" Assume the answer is 30%. The next question is, "By how many minutes, on average, are orders late?" Assume the answer is 10 minutes. You would then know the specific condition needing remedy is: "30% of our orders are served 10 minutes late." By quantifying the condition, you will understand what is really happening, allowing you to ask questions that can lead to the most appropriate solution, such as, "If we can't eliminate late deliveries, how can we cut them down to 15%?" or "If our late deliveries are as high as 50%, are we making unrealistic promises to our guests?" Quantifying with real numbers is far more valuable than approximating. Approximations might simply reinforce inaccurate perceptions.

In other words, through actual quantification, you might discover a very different condition than you thought existed.

"The hospitality industry executive's perceptions of the quality of their organization's products and services are far rosier (70%) than the perceptions of the people who paid to be served (40%)."

–Training Magazine June 1993

McDonald's Predictability

Standardized and uniform services are predictable which means that no matter where a person goes, they will receive the same service and receive the same product every time when interacting with the McDonaldized organization.

This also applies to the workers in those organizations. Their tasks are highly repetitive, highly routine, and predictable.

A Big Mac is a Big Mac is a Big Mac.

Profitability System Outline:

Goal: To meet or exceed guests' enjoyment expectations.

Quality: "*Doing the right thing right, the first time, on time, all the time, and always to the guest's satisfaction.*"

Value: The guest's judgment of the usefulness of the service or product based on their perceptions of the enjoyment they received, and the time and money spent.

Typical "Unique" Restaurant Profitability Systems:

Financial: Sales receipts, accounting, cash control, statements, inventory, purchasing, accounts payable, cash flow, and payroll.

Service: Hosting, serving, and collection.

Production: Baking, food batch cooking, grilling recipes, and dishwashing.

Systems to Ensure Guest Satisfaction

Greet and Thank Guests: Ensure guests feel welcome and appreciated.

Fast Service Systems: Include "Pre-Assign Tables," "Seat Servers in Rotation," "Clarify Order," "Utilize All Seating While On-A-Wait," "Coordinate Seating While on a Wait," "Communicate by Radio," "Assign Servers to Sections," "Serve Next Order Up," "Care for and Use of Table Seating," "Expedite Orders," and "Supervising" systems.

Friendly Service Systems: Include "Friendly Servfast™ Table Service," "Select Staff Member for Server Position," "Manage Servers," "Use Telephone Etiquette," and "Assist Callers with Questions."

Theft and Pilferage Prevention: Include "Audit Guest Check Accuracy," "Manage Staff Member Entrance," "Cash Drawer Reconciliation," and "Prepare and Make a Bank Deposit" systems.

Cleanliness Systems: Include "Cleanliness Inspection System," "Custodial Duties Checklist," "Clean and Sanitize Restrooms," "Use of Gray Cleaning Buckets and Bar Towels," "Sweep Floors," "Care and Use of Floor Mops," and "Department Opening and Closing Checklists."

Festive Atmosphere Care Systems: Include "Custodial and Dining Room Cleaning and Dusting Systems."

Cost and Waste Minimization: Include "Controlling Receiving, Storing, Food Portioning, and Materials and Utility Waste Systems." Minimize labor costs through "Scheduling," "Hustle," and "Management of Systems."

SYSTEM MANAGEMENT STANDARDS

Standards: There can be no improvement where there are no standards. The starting point in any improvement is to know exactly where one stands. There must be a precise standard of measurement. Every standard and measurement cries out for constant support, revision, and upgrading.

Discipline: Standards must be binding on everyone. It is management's job to see that everyone works according to the established steps and standards.

Quality Focus: Management must constantly focus on the quality of results. As competitors provide better products and services, any restaurant providing less than the best will be driven out of existence. Guests demand this quality through their buying habits.

Leadership: Good leaders display a commitment to guest enjoyment, an interest in individuals, excitement for activity, a thirst for knowledge and advancement, and a willingness to try new approaches and techniques. They are problem solvers through profitability system improvement and never seem over-challenged with the work.

Continuous Improvement: Improvements and innovations are constantly needed on production and service systems rather than on specific problems. Simply solving issues as they arise is not sufficient; the overall approach needs to be improved.

Education and Training: Initiate programs of education, ongoing orientation, and retraining. With today's rapid pace of change, facts and techniques quickly become outdated. Company and industry information should be broadly shared with staff members.

Driving Without Fear: Profitability system management based on continuous improvement necessitates continual change. Fear inhibits change. The opposite of fear is trust.

Breaking Down Barriers: All barriers between departments are dysfunctional and must be broken down. Managers play an especially critical role in eliminating hostilities and abolishing fear. Each person is required to assist others in the process of providing delicious food and fast, friendly service in a clean, festive atmosphere.

Self-Inspection: The producing staff is responsible for inspecting their work as well as the work of all others. Staff members are trained to refuse to serve products that do not meet standards.

Pride in Workmanship: Profitability systems must reward staff members for doing more than the established standard by recognizing them for improving the profitability system. Empowerment means giving staff members the authority to suggest changes to systems.

Eliminating Quotas: Quotas often become the minimum and maximum level of acceptable performance. Any product or service standard below 100% is unacceptable and must be continuously challenged and improved.

Eliminating Slogans: Staff members will never be asked to accept slogans and targets unless they are given sufficient guidelines and facilitating changes. Management must facilitate substantial system change to achieve the desired perfection.

Taking Action: "*Do it.*" Whatever errors are made in system management, they are likely to be less costly than the status quo. Every journey begins with a step.

RECOMMENDING PROFITABILITY SYSTEM IMPROVEMENTS

The person using a profitability system is in the best position to improve it. To fully participate in a restaurant operation, staff must go beyond merely following systems. Every system requires continuous improvement to enhance the guest's positive experience and control business costs. To effectively compete in the future, you must improve your operation. Encourage your staff members to assume ownership of restaurant operations and perform strategic work by improving current profitability systems.

Never assume you've got it all figured out because your guests or competitors will eventually out-figure you. If you think you've made it idiot-proof, someone will always make a better idiot.

Predetermine your operational results by creating them through the development and modification of practical profitability systems. Ask yourself the following questions regarding your current systems:

Should the result/objective be changed?

Does the current system best meet all the guest's needs?

Have guests' needs changed?

Can something be eliminated?

Does each step add value?

Is there any duplication?

Can different methods, technology, or equipment be used?

Can fewer costly materials or services be used?

Can the time it takes be reduced?

Is there a simpler way to achieve the same result?

Are instructions complete and easy to understand?

What would the perfect process be?

Can something be rearranged?

Is the layout and sequence the most efficient?

Can any systems be combined?

Is there a need to continually remind staff members of the same issues with a system?

IMPLEMENTING CHANGES IN OPERATING SYSTEMS

Changing or introducing a new system constitutes a change in the Position Agreement between the restaurant and each affected staff member. Each change must be clear to the staff member to establish new accountability. Ensure every staff member understands and fulfills changes to their position contract accountabilities.

Have affected staff members read the new or revised system according to the *"Tell E'm"* Training System on their next shift.

Demonstrate the techniques and have them perform the system according to the *"Show E'm"* Training System.

Have your subordinate demonstrate the system correctly to you according to the *"Check E'm"* Training System.

Have them sign on a list of affected staff members.

Review the change with any staff member observed not doing it correctly. Provide verbal correction as needed.

Verify Profitability System Implementation

The result of a system could be: System implementation is verified in a manner that ensures it has been trained to each affected staff member and manager.

Randomly test a number of staff members for compliance with the new/improved profitability system.

Sign, date, and list the staff members tested on the System Implementation Form.

Initial the ok'd space when you witness staff performing the stated system correctly.

Make adjustments as necessary to the system.

Determine the cause when a new profitability system is not being followed by asking the following questions: Was adequate testing performed before implementing the system? Did management provide adequate training and supervision?

DELIVER A QUALITY RESTAURANT EXPERIENCE

A quality restaurant experience is whatever your guests say it is. It is changing and evolving. You must be committed to providing your staff members and guests with a quality experience every day. Quality is a dance between effective systems and dedicated staff members. It is your ability to deliver exactness with precision—absolutely without compromise, hour by hour, day in and day out. Quality requires the integrity and commitment of involved staff members to do what your restaurant does better than anyone else. Providing quality products and services to guests gives your staff a sense of pride and accomplishment. Quality is about your ability to conceive, develop, and produce products and services that do what no other restaurant does in a way that satisfies guests' needs consistently and predictably every time. See your restaurant as a "Quality Machine."

You can achieve the ultimate quality of products and services by building quantification, objective measurements, and evaluation into your ongoing business processes. This requires achieving "Perfect information flow."

Quality Bandits:

Defending the status quo

Lack of information

Subjectivity of perception

Lying

Solutions

Communicate expectations clearly and directly.

Look for systemic solutions to problems rather than blaming people.

Make systems easily accessible to management and staff members.

Be aware of your blind spots.

Use people's mistakes as learning opportunities.

Do not jump to conclusions based on limited information.

Ask more questions and seek out other sides of the story.

"Eighty percent of customers' frustrations come from bad systems, not bad people."- John Goodman, business consultant.

Consider ISO 9000 Accreditation

Although we never intended to receive ISO 9000 accreditation, we adopted the principles of ISO 9000. We worked to ensure our operation was 100% documented and that we were very reliable in executing our systems for our Guest's Enjoyment.

"In manufacturing, ISO is a measure of excellence or a state of being free from defects, deficiencies and significant variations. It is brought about by strict and consistent commitment to certain standards that achieve uniformity of a product in order to satisfy specific customer or user requirements. ISO 8402-1986 standard defines quality as "the totality of features and characteristics of a product or service that bears its ability to satisfy stated or implied needs." If an automobile company finds a defect in one of their cars and makes a product recall, customer reliability and therefore production will decrease because trust will be lost in the car's quality."

–www.businessdictionary.com

An ISO 9000-qualified restaurant company has systems in place that create an enjoyable eating and drinking experience for guests *every time* and does it profitably. The ISO 9000 family of quality management systems standards is designed to help organizations ensure that they meet the needs of guests and other stakeholders while meeting statutory and regulatory requirements related to a product.

ISO 9000 deals with the fundamentals of quality management systems, including the eight management principles upon which the family of standards is based. ISO 9001 deals with the requirements that organizations wishing to meet the standard must fulfill.

The ISO 9000 Series is based on Eight Quality Management Principles, which include:

Principle 1 – Customer focus.

Organizations depend on their customers and therefore should understand current and future customer needs, should meet customer requirements, and strive to exceed customer expectations.

Principle 2 – Leadership.

Leaders establish unity of purpose and direction of the organization. They should create and maintain the internal environment in which people can become fully involved in achieving the organization's objectives.

Principle 3 – Involvement of people.

People at all levels are the essence of an organization and their full involvement enables their abilities to be used for the organization's benefit.

Principle 4 – Process approach.

A desired result is achieved more efficiently when activities are managed as a process.

Principle 5 – System approach to management.

Identifying, understanding, and managing interrelated processes as a system contributes to the organization's effectiveness and efficiency in achieving its objectives.

Principle 6 – Continual improvement.

Continual improvement of the organization's overall performance should be a permanent objective of the organization.

Principle 7 – Factual approach to decision making.

Effective decisions are based on the analysis of data and information.

Principle 8 – Mutually beneficial supplier relationships.

An organization and its suppliers are interdependent, and a mutually beneficial relationship enhances the ability of both to create value. –Wikipedia ISO 9000.

Adopt the Kaizen Philosophy

The Kaizen philosophy of operating aims to eliminate waste by improving standardized activities and processes. Kaizen was first implemented in several Japanese businesses after the Second World War, influenced in part by American business and quality management teachers who visited the country. It has since spread throughout the world and is now being implemented outside of business.

Improve Daily: Try to improve something at your restaurant every day. Look for things that need improvement or change to reduce costs or increase sales.

Visualize Competition: Visualize that competing restaurants are improving, and you need to stay ahead of them.

Avoid Complacency: Never be complacent about your leading position in the market.

Prepare for New Competitors: Imagine a new competing restaurant will soon be coming to town with better décor, food, service, location, and cleanliness. Improve your restaurant now to stay ahead.

A Kaizen business strategy calls for never-ending efforts for improvement. Continual change to existing standards and systems is essential for your long-term success. By asking what you can do today to meet your guests' needs better, you demonstrate your willingness to question your work methods constantly. Focus on numerous small improvements to enhance your restaurant's performance continuously. Question your ways of doing things and strive to improve work processes. Achieve continuous improvement through the systematic pursuit of guest enjoyment by innovating, quantifying, and orchestrating.

Innovation: Conceiving and implementing a new way of achieving a result or performing work. Taking corrective measures, if necessary, to ensure progress is maintained.

Quantification: Checking and measuring results to confirm whether the objective has been attained.

Orchestration: Establishing by documentation a routine way of performing work so desired results can be consistently achieved.

Repeat: Innovation - Quantification - Orchestration to continuously develop an extraordinary business.

Constant Improvement is the Way of Operating, Day In and Day Out

Change is the one constant in life. In business, you change and improve, or you go out of business. The market you serve is changing, and your staff members are changing. Embrace change and improve for the better.

"Kaizen is a daily process, the purpose of which goes beyond simple productivity improvement. It is also a process that, when done correctly, humanizes the workplace, eliminates overly hard work ('muri'), and teaches people how to perform experiments on their work using the scientific method and how to learn to spot and eliminate waste in business processes. In all, the process suggests a humanized approach to workers and to increasing productivity: 'The idea is to nurture the company's people as much as it is to praise and encourage participation in kaizen activities.' Successful implementation requires 'the participation of workers in the improvement.' People at all levels of an organization participate in kaizen, from the CEO down to janitorial staff, as well as external stakeholders when applicable."

–Wikipedia

You are constantly faced with new competition and rising guest expectations. If you're coasting, you're going downhill. You probably do not own any patents, secrets, or franchise agreements that give you a unique advantage over your competition. All you have is the desire to do your best at being your best. It is your secret weapon. Ensure your growth by continually questioning your work and developing better methods. Strive to "get it right" every day. Make small improvements daily. Change quickly when a better method is found. Create what isn't by consistently following your systems day by day.

Another Quality Definition: "Doing the right thing (the guest's requirements), right the first time, every time, on time, and always to the guest's satisfaction."

PERFORM QUALITY ASSURANCE OF YOUR SYSTEMS

The objective of quality assurance is to provide the restaurant operator with information regarding the performance and emotional state of personnel and to verify that the company's restaurant is operating according to systems. Make recommendations for corrective measures to improve systems and achieve better results.

Start with a copy of the systems, rules, and standards to be examined.

Go to the station where the system is being performed.

Observe step-by-step the work, from an out-of-the-way place, performing the systems.

Move around your restaurant to avoid becoming the focus of attention.

Communicate with staff members about the system's results, steps, and standards as needed. Many suggestions for system improvements can be learned.

Summarize all observations with the responsible manager at the appropriate time.

Turn in the completed examination to the appropriate management.

The manager/supervisor of the department is the quality control person. The quality review person is not in control of processes; they are only a reporter. The operator responsible for the entire restaurant will be informed of the outcomes of the quality review results.

Protect Your Systems and Operating Manuals

It's wise to protect the intellectual property that you develop. All of the systems, methods, processes, and procedures that you produce should be retained solely for you and your organization. Identify your copyright with a statement at the bottom of each document, such as:

"This document is confidential and proprietary to (your organization's legal name) and cannot be used or duplicated without the consent of (your organization's legal name). This is an unpublished work protected by federal copyright laws, and no unauthorized copying, adaptation, distribution, or display is permitted."

FOURTH KEY TO $UCCESS
PROVIDE CLEAN, SAFE AND SANITARY FACILITIES

First and Foremost, Guests Require Your Restaurant to be Safe, Clean, and Sanitary.

A clean restaurant attracts guests, as even the mere thought of possibly getting sick from eating at an unclean restaurant will keep people away. Guests look for indicators of your sanitation practices in various areas, including:

Having an immaculate restaurant is a challenge when dealing with hundreds of guests. They and their children may spill food, touch surfaces with greasy hands, track dirt, and make other messes. Cleaning up after guests is part of the restaurant business. Teaching your staff to be sensitive to guest messes and clean them up promptly is crucial.

Your cleanliness strategy should surprise and attract guests back with cleaner facilities, more smartly dressed staff members, and sanitary conditions. Aim to be cleaner than your competition and cleaner than you used to be, demonstrating that you and your staff are committed to the guest enjoyment project.

Never expose your guests to germs, food poisoning risks, or visible issues such as fingerprints, dust, smudges, crumbs, litter, soil, stains, grime, worn surfaces, broken equipment, or evidence of previous guests at their table. Everything in your restaurant must create a cleanliness event for them.

People avoid restaurants they perceive as unsanitary or dirty due to fears of germs and disease-causing conditions. Your facilities must be perceived as safe, uncluttered, spotlessly clean, sanitary, and free from dirt, soil, stains, and grime. Words like immaculate, sparkling, new, bright, and safe should come to mind when describing your restaurant.

Reassure guests that one of the reasons your restaurant is their best choice is its cleanliness and sanitary conditions, surpassing those of competing restaurants. This starts from your parking lot, front doors, and windows, extending to every part of your restaurant. A clean and sanitary environment is a fundamental requirement. If your restaurant isn't clean and hygienic, nothing else matters. Many people judge the cleanliness of a restaurant according to their judgment of the cleanliness and sanitation of the restrooms.

Cleaning Responsibilities:

- Staff members must wash their hands when coming on duty, after using the restroom, and throughout each shift.

- Thoroughly clean the top, sides, and edges of everything in workstations.

Safety Concerns:

- Design facilities with safety features such as handrails for stairs and clearly lighted and well-marked steps.

- Equip facilities with fire alarms, clearly identified exits, and conveniently located fire extinguishers.

- Use nonskid surfaces on floors and mark spills on floors.

- Post room occupancy limits.

By focusing on these aspects, you can create a safe and clean environment that attracts guests and ensures their continued safety and patronage.

Install Systems, Schedules, and Training to Ensure Restaurant Cleanliness, Sanitation, and Safety Standards remain excellent throughout your open hours.

- **Create a weekly or monthly cleaning inspection form for every area of your restaurant.** This close examination is essential to maintaining a spotlessly clean restaurant. Include every square foot of your restaurant facility inside and outside. Inspect every piece of equipment, every room, every seating area, evert restroom, every storage room, every kitchen. Mark it as clean without dust, grit, smudge or dirty. Score the results as a percentage clean and post it for all to see. Have unclean areas cleaned.

- **Exterior Cleanliness:** Ensure the restaurant parking lot, street gutters, trash dumpster area, landscape, sidewalks, and entry are free of soil, litter, weeds, and disrepair. Keep walkways and parking areas free of snow and ice during inclement weather. Survey the exterior hourly to ensure the exterior areas remain attractive. Ensure your receiving door porch is clean and free of stains and debris.

- **Windows and Doors:** Schedule doors and window glass shining, free of fingerprints and smudges.

- **Floors:** Maintain floors and floor coverings in spotless, like-new condition. Clean carpets on a scheduled basis.

- **Lighting:** Ensure lighting fixtures are clean and fully operational. Ensure exterior lighting is off during daylight hours.

- **Lobby:** Maintain a tidy and welcoming lobby area.

- **Safe Conditions:** Ensure all conditions are safe for staff members and guests.

- **Floor Spills Safety:** Clearly mark floor spills and other hazards. Identify spills with caution signs. Clean spills immediately.

- **Stairs Safety:** Clearly mark stairs and equip them with handrails. Hosts should clearly identify stairs and spills while seating guests.

- **Safety Equipment:** Secure fire alarms, fire suppressors in cooking areas, and extinguishers in accessible places, and conduct regular inspections.

- **Food Safety:** Clean or dispose of food that touches an unsanitary surface.

- **Interior Cleanliness:** Keep entry areas, dining areas, seating, HVAC grills, and wall displays and décor free of dust, visible wear, disrepair, soil, and smudges.

- **Restrooms:** Clean restroom toilets and urinals daily with the proper sanitization materials. Maintain restroom floors, walls, ceilings, mirrors, fixtures, fans, and vents in spotlessly clean condition. Make hourly cleaning checks to keep restrooms in spotless condition throughout your open hours. Keep restroom paper supplies well-stocked, soap dispensers operating, and trash emptied.

- **Dining Area:** Ensure tabletops and condiment holders are clean and free of fingerprints, maintaining a like-new condition. Décor is attractive and enjoyable to look at.

- **Seating:** Maintain well-constructed and comfortable seating. Upholstered seats should be in good condition, with no cracking or signs of wear and tear.

- Kitchen Areas: Keep kitchen areas spotless and organized.

- **Food Storage:** Store foods and supplies front-facing, six inches off the floor, on pallets or shelving to prevent contamination or water damage. Rotate purchased and prepared foods using the FIFO method.

- **Refrigeration:** Maintain refrigerators below 40°F and freezers below 0°F.

- **Dishwashing:** Ensure soiled dishes, glassware, flatware, utensils, and pans are washed, cleaned, and sanitized.

- **Workstations:** Keep workstations clean and organized. Ensure there is an assigned place for everything and everything is in its place.

- **Trash and Dirty Dishes:** Dispose of trash immediately and take dirty dishes directly to the dishwasher.

- **Sanitary Handling:** Handle glasses, dishes, flatware, and utensils in a sanitary manner to avoid spreading germs. Never touch the rim of a glass or fork tines where mouths touch.

- **Staff Hygiene and Appearance:** Ensure staff members present a clean appearance, with good hygiene, brushed teeth, daily baths, use of deodorant, and wearing clean undergarments, including clean aprons and uniforms.

- **Cleanliness Touchpoints:** Ensure menus, condiment containers, shakers, chairs, and tables feel clean to the touch. Ensure handrails and door handles are clean to the guest's touch. Buffet plates and glassware should also be clean to the guest's touch.

Clean dirt is a spill or smudge that just happened. Dirty dirt is a spill or smudge allowed to remain beyond a reasonable time. Keep your restaurant clean by removing "clean dirt" before it becomes "dirty dirt."

FIFTH KEY TO $UCCESS
DELIVER FAST, FRIENDLY SERVICE

Guests Enjoy Fast, Friendly Hospitality. Your Restaurant Must Provide Your Guests a Fast, Friendly Hospitality Service Experience.

DEVELOP YOUR "ENJOYMENT" SERVICE SYSTEMS

Ensure your staff members are welcoming, attractive, friendly, well-mannered, prompt, helpful, and appreciative. Guests expect pleasant, well-mannered social interactions, friendly service, and appreciation for their patronage. They expect to be treated with respect, like royalty.

Developing an excellent service process is one way to wow your guests. Exceeding in friendly and professional service is a critical way to surpass your guests' expectations. Every staff member must be accountable for displaying a positive, helpful attitude toward guests. Courtesy and consideration are expected at a minimum. Many staff members may not have strong manners, so they must be trained to ensure value for your restaurant. Staff responses to predictable and unpredictable occurrences need to be spelled out in your systems.

Standardized Greeting

Your restaurant service should include a standardized greeting such as "Welcome to Peppers." This is a chance to differentiate your restaurant from competitors. Tired receptions from untrained staff members are boring and do not convey a strong welcome. Standard greetings like "Two tonight" or "How many" are unexciting. Server should also give new guests an outgoing, energetic, and enthusiastic greeting. Cashiers, servers, and hosts should provide a sincere "thank you" and a smile to guests who are leaving.

Attractive Uniforms

Staff members should be dressed attractively in clean, stylish uniforms. People perform better when they look sharp. Uniforms create a favorable impression on guests, making staff members appear organized and part of a unified team. A clean, well-maintained uniform positively affects staff members' attitudes. Uniforms should be kept spotless during shifts, and nametags should be worn to help establish a friendly connection between staff and guests.

Assistance and Attention to Needs

Staff should make it a habit to assist guests and pay attention to their needs. Promptness is key. Staff your restaurant to provide consistent service during both slower and busier times. The challenge is to match the number of staff members with the number of guests at any given time. Too few staff members can lead to chaos, while too many can result in excessive labor costs. Well-trained staff should avoid delays by not engaging in personal conversations or providing unfocused service.

PROVIDE GUESTS FRIENDLINESS AND SOCIABILITY

Friendliness includes showing guests kindness and goodwill. Teach your staff to be attentive, congenial, and receptive to guests' needs. They should radiate friendliness and sociability.

Your staff's appearance is one form of practicing manners and an essential sign of consideration and respect. Staff members must be taught good old-fashioned manners and professional service techniques. Manners are becoming less common in today's marketplace. Being courteous and friendly to guests makes them feel appreciated and welcome to your restaurant. A polite and helpful service is essential and may differentiate your operation from your competition. Your staff should express appreciation for guests' patronage, which provides them with their paychecks and your restaurant's success.

Expressing gratitude for your guests' patronage is a vital ingredient in your service recipe. Being thankful is appreciated by your guests. When a guest says thank you for some service, staff should respond with "my pleasure" instead of the modern, negative and all too common "no problem" or "of course."

Occasionally, you may have staff members who are easily distracted, feeling down, or overwhelmed with their workload. Some people may have personal problems that affect their work. Staff members must never be unfriendly or seem unhappy to see guests. They may mistakenly think that getting guests to return is not their job and that they play an insignificant role in the process. They need to understand their responsibilities in bringing guests back tomorrow. Your staff should never, ever cause guests to feel irritated by being ignored or unappreciated. People are attracted back to restaurants where the staff is friendly and shows appreciation for their patronage. They avoid places where they do not receive friendly treatment. Guests expect to be treated like they are important, with politeness and respect. Not every person you hire will be naturally friendly. You must train your staff in proper behavior and expect them to be friendly and genuinely happy that guests have come to your restaurant.

One additional way to show common courtesy to your guests is to accommodate those whose watches are slightly slow or fast. Whatever their time problem is, you can be extra accommodating by opening your restaurant doors five minutes earlier and closing five minutes later than your posted hours of operation. It can be frustrating to pull on a business door and find it locked when you are only a few minutes early or late.

Your staff should exhibit enthusiasm while serving guests and make their needs, spoken or unspoken, their number one priority. They should convince guests that they are happy to have them for the restaurant experience. Your staff should focus on the positive rather than personal or non-work-related problems. Above all, they must provide an enjoyable restaurant experience for guests. Being friendly towards guests and other staff members is a non-negotiable requirement and a standard for any successful and growing restaurant.

Your restaurant should be known for its friendly staff members. Guests' perceptions are established every time your staff contacts them. Friendliness is a natural result of genuinely liking and caring for people. Your restaurant will be seen as neighborly, attentive, and festive. Your staff should seek opportunities to make friendly eye contact with guests and assist them. Make guest needs, wants, and requests, spoken or unspoken, their number one priority.

Excellent manners can help you have better relationships with people you know and those you will meet. Politeness may be defined as the management of your words and actions, whereby you make other people have a better opinion of you and themselves.

GOOD MANNERS AND CONSIDERATION

Your business is all about serving the needs of your guests. Putting them first and treating them well is a basic requirement and opportunity for your business. Each interaction with guests—greeting them, seating them, serving them, collecting from them, and bidding them farewell—is vital to their experience.

Displaying good manners and showing consideration for guests is not an optional ingredient in the restaurant business.

"Good manners are just a way of showing other people that we have respect for them."

–Bill Kelly, writer-actor

Manners Quotes by: James Allen 19th century Philosopher – *Mind is the Master*

"Children who are well-bred are taught always to consider the happiness of others before their own: to offer them the best seat, the choicest fruit, the best tidbit, and so on; and also, to do everything, even the most trivial acts, in the right way."

"And these two things – unselfishness and right action – are at the basis, not only of good manners, but of all ethics, religion, and true living: they represent power and skill. The selfish person is weak and unskillful in the exercise of thought. The vulgar person is weak and unskillful in their actions. Unselfishness is the right way of thinking; good manners are the right way of acting."

"The cultivation of good manners plays an important part in your success. Poor manners and their corrosive influence will eat into all your efforts, and disfigure your happiness and prosperity, as powerful acid eats into and disfigures the finest steel."

"The right-doer will avoid those acts of personal pleasure and gratification, which by their nature bring annoyance, pain, or suffering to others, no matter how insignificant those actions may appear to be."

Install Systems, Schedules, and Training to Ensure the Restaurant's Friendly Hospitality Service Standards Are Met; Making Guests Feel at Ease is the Essence of Staff Etiquette

- A warm smile and eye contact is are the universal language of welcome. A smiling, pleasant, and enthusiastic attitude is essential.

- There are few words more elementary or appreciated than "please" and "thank you."

- Speak softly and politely; your voice reflects your character.

- Speak properly. Make it a habit to pronounce your words and use correct grammar.

- Speak clearly; refrain from mumbling or speaking too fast.

- Avoid slang and calling people by pet names or short forms unless you are close to them.

- Do not gossip or pry. Do not ask personal or intrusive questions of guests.

- Good moods are contagious; hopefully, yours will be pleasantly catching.

- Groom yourself appropriately and do it in private (hair, nose, ears, teeth, and hands).

- Never underestimate the message that is sent by your appearance, poise, and posture.

- Bathe often; wear freshly laundered clothes and deodorant.

- Coughing and sneezing into your elbow shows consideration for others.

- A short fuse does nothing but burn; if you find yourself with one, steer clear.

- Let common sense be your guide and graciousness your goal.

- Try to make as little noise as possible in all situations, especially when bussing a dirty table of dishes and glassware.

- Staff members must display friendly body language and maintain good posture.

- Staff members should make and hold eye contact during guest interactions and show genuine smiles with appropriate facial expressions.

- Every person is important and deserves consideration and respect. Staff members should avoid disturbing others with loud laughter, loud talking, and making noises.

- Don't noisily talk or laugh; crack your knuckles or neck.

- Manners are a courtesy, telling guests they are important and you care about them.

- Always treat guests with kindness.

- Exhibit a helpful attitude, a pleasant personality, and a desire to serve.

- Stand and walk tall. Never slouch or walk slovenly.

- Never touch guests (many people have a comfort zone, and touching is often perceived as invasive).

- Don't cross your arms in front of you; it means "do not disturb me."

- Stand facing guests and look for an opportunity to provide service.

- Stop and give guests the right of way. Stand aside for them to pass.

- Don't point in the dining room; it is impolite because it distracts other guests.

- Escort inquiring guests to the restrooms and exit, etc.

- Don't waste time or sit down in front of guests.

- Be alert and attentive to guests' needs.

- Avoid self-indulgences like combing or touching your hair, scratching, primping your appearance, or drinking or eating in guests' view.

- Be patient with guests who exhibit poor manners.

- Always give guests priority over your personal conversations and cleaning.

PROVIDE PROFESSIONAL FULL HOSPITALITY TABLE SERVICE

Good full service in a restaurant includes providing guests with time-honored service techniques. These include how to greet, take orders, serve orders, remove dirty dishes, present guest checks, and express appreciation for the guests' business.

- Take the drink order soon after guests first sit down, beginning with ladies.

- Write orders in a sequential order corresponding to the seats on your order pad to avoid auctioning food off at the table. Know who ordered what item without asking.

- Take the women's food order first, followed by the men and children. Serve older people at the beginning.

- Make appropriate suggestions for specials and appetizers. "May I suggest our... soup?"

- Clarify orders by saying, "May I repeat your order, please?" This eliminates misunderstanding and ensures correct order preparation.

- Thank guests politely for their orders and collect the menus.

- Present the drink and food in an appetizing manner as soon as possible.

- Always use a tray to carry food and beverages to and from the table.

- Serve beverages to guests' right hands from their right side using your right hand.

- Serve food from the guests' left, using your left hand, and clear from their right, using your right hand.

- Place each item in front of the correct guest, taking care to avoid spills.

- Warn guests to be cautious with hot plates and when seated near stairs.

- Ask a coworker for assistance when serving large orders of food.

- Do not talk or cough over food and drinks.

- Handle glasses, plates, and flatware properly. Never touch the rim of a glass where guests put their mouths. Handle wine glasses by their stems and silverware by the handles.

- Always serve (1) drinks, (2) appetizers, (3) entrees, and (4) desserts at the same time.

- Never leave one guest hungry while everyone else is enjoying their food.

- Never reach across one guest to serve another.

- Avoid bumping into tables or chairs.

- Never clear a plate full of food without asking if there is anything wrong with it. When something is wrong with a meal, try to fix it.

- When refilling water or wine glasses, refill them without touching the glass.

- Never interrupt guests' conversations unnecessarily. Perform your services quietly.

- Make a pleasant dessert inquiry before guests finish their meal.

- Present the guest check promptly to avoid causing them any delay when they are ready to leave.

- Express appreciation for guests coming.

- Write a quick thank-you note on the back of their check.

- Never put your hands into your pocket, sit, or lean on counters.

- Be ready to respond to a guest's need!

- Stay in good physical condition to maintain high energy throughout each shift.

- If you can't talk and work simultaneously, don't talk.

PROVIDE GUESTS FAST SERVICE

Guests enjoy fast service. Guests require you to be productive. Your restaurant can't be too quick. Guests are often in a hurry and become frustrated when their time is being wasted, or they experience unnecessary delays. The line between full and fast service is blurred in many guests' minds, causing full-service units to compete with fast food and fast casual units.

Providing extra fast service is another way to exceed guests' expectations. While guests may accept normal service speed, they are impressed when it's faster than expected. Planning the correct staff schedule is critical in providing impressive, fast service. Anything that slows down your service process detracts from the guest experience.

Anytime your guests are waiting beyond a reasonable time for service or food, you are "in the weeds." These risky situations call for an all-hands-on-deck action to correct the waiting conditions. Guests may be waiting to be seated, waiting to have their order taken, waiting for their order, waiting for their check, or waiting to pay. These are critical times that impact your guests' image of your restaurant. This condition must be corrected

ASAP to save your restaurant's image. Your staff members must be aware that no matter what their challenges are in serving guests, most guests have a prompt service requirement.

Stamp out service and production delays. Minimize the time guests have to wait. Plan and use your staff's time well during slow periods to prepare for busy periods. Eliminating all "in the weeds" conditions is critical.

People have come to expect instant service from restaurants. They will not use a restaurant that does not provide fast service. Their time is valuable to them. Quick service is essential for an enjoyable experience.

"A well-run restaurant is like a winning baseball team. It makes the most of every crew member's talent and takes advantage of every split-second opportunity to speed up service."

–David Ogilvy, British advertising tycoon

My First and My Last JB's Big Boy Restaurant Experience.

My first JB's restaurant experience was when I was first in business. I went to a newly opened restaurant for lunch. This was back in 1962 when speedy service was not too common in restaurants in our area. It was JB's Big Boy Restaurant's first location in Utah. They had taken over the site of a failed restaurant called the Ivory Tower in Provo. Even after 60 years, I remember the experience vividly.

We were seated immediately upon arriving despite the restaurant being busy. I was surprised when the server promptly approached our table with menus. She took our order straight away, and, to my astonishment, our order was served within a few short minutes. The server inquired about our satisfaction with the meal and presented our check. The speed and efficiency of the service made me realize that we needed to become more efficient with our service, or we risked losing business to new competition.

Over the next few months, we improved our service processes, becoming faster and more efficient. It's essential to stay aware of your competition and their operational methods and products. You can learn many valuable lessons from them that can help improve your restaurant.

My last JB's Restaurants experience was in Cedar City, Utah, in 2007, where I encountered how chaotic a restaurant can become. It was breakfast time, and I remember the experience as if it were yesterday. There was a shortage of servers and cooks, resulting in long waits for service and food. The manager was frantically moving around the dining room, trying to calm guests and apologize for the delays. The entire restaurant was in chaos, and it seemed almost every table of guests was upset about their experience. I felt sorry for the manager, who was clearly overwhelmed by the situation.

PROVIDE A FAST AND EFFICIENT RESTAURANT EXPERIENCE

Service efficiency variations can and do happen regularly in the restaurant business. The inconsistent flow of guests is a significant challenge. Matching the number of guests with an appropriate number of staff members to provide efficient service is tricky. This can be due to poor planning when anticipating the number of guests who show up or call in on any given shift. Using last year's sales pattern is helpful in projecting sales. There can be a shortage of staff due to not hiring when needed, a limited labor market, staff members calling in sick, misunderstandings about schedules, or no-shows for a shift. New staff members and trainees cannot handle the workload like they will after a few weeks on the job. These factors can cause guests delays in receiving their expected and required service.

One essential organizational strategy is to have a good number of your staff cross-trained in other positions. Train some dining staff to assist in the kitchen when kitchen work demands are high, and dining demands are less challenging, and vice versa. Have your office staff trained to assist during heavy lunch pressure and management ready to help wherever excessive demand periods occur. Organize so everyone on duty is equally challenged during heavy demand periods. General management must see service breaking points and coordinate staff so the guest receives the fastest service possible under all conditions.

Your fast service strategy should be to pleasantly surprise and attract guests back with faster service. Never make a guest endure amateur service or suffer a wait to be seated, a delay in having their order taken and served, or experience unnecessary delays in paying. Faster service means faster than you were yesterday and/or faster than your competition. Everything in your restaurant must help create efficient and prompt events for your guests.

Providing faster service requires being organized and prepared. Fast is moving with ease and quickness, taking a comparatively short time to accomplish work. Speed, like quality, takes time to develop. "In the weeds" is a term used when a restaurant is providing slow or disorganized service.

Fast service responsibilities include such things as staff members speeding up service to guests and other staff members they serve! (Such as cooks serving servers and prep serving kitchen staff.) Astonish your guests with your efficient work. Your staff members should first concentrate on doing their job correctly and then increase their work speed day by day.

Work on your staff producing more in less time while still maintaining your exacting high-quality standards. They should work quickly during slow periods to avoid falling behind during busy periods. This will make them more valuable by reducing production costs for the restaurant. Make part of your restaurant's culture to work quickly and efficiently.

Ensure staff members are working fast without being unsafe to themselves or others. They should use elbow grease and do handwork quickly and carefully. Moving quickly and never distracting or disrupting others' work should be a goal.

While moving around the restaurant, everyone should stay to the right, not block aisles or stand with elbows out. Another important way of providing fast service to guests is concentrating on the work. Your staff should avoid distractions and disruptions that slow their productivity; avoid confusion and wasting time with unnecessary conversation and activities. Everyone must be alert and attentive to guests' needs.

Management and staff should exhibit a high sense of urgency! Don't give the appearance that you are bored or unprepared to respond immediately with a sense of urgency.

Advice to Your Staff

Most staff members want to be productive, though many have not experienced high productivity. Productivity improves with good coaching and work experience. Restaurant work is fast-paced, requiring good manual dexterity and agility. Labor cost is one measure of productivity. It usually represents the single largest cost to a restaurant and must be minimized to maintain a profitable operation. The number of dollars each staff member produces per hour must continually be monitored and improved. High labor costs are a result of low productivity. Restaurants often provide better service when pressed for time than when staff members have time to socialize.

THE TRADITIONAL SERVER-COOK CONFLICT

Quite often, conflicts arise in a restaurant between servers in the dining room and cooks in the kitchen. Servers may become anxious about where their food is and complain to the cooks. The problem is that servers are face-to-face with guests, whereas cooks are usually away from them and feel they are doing their best to produce the food. The kitchen staff may be shorthanded and need assistance or may have developed their own pace standard for speed of service. As management, you must be sensitive to the problem and schedule more cooks during times of slower kitchen service. It is preferable to have a timing system in the kitchen so cooks and management can monitor actual kitchen production times. This is the only accurate measurement of the speed of kitchen service in a restaurant. Eliminating slow service times is essential for a successful restaurant operation.

Fast service has become an essential part of guests having an enjoyable experience at restaurants. Guests are often in a hurry, and their time is valuable to them. They have come to expect and require instantaneous service. The marketplace is providing them with faster and faster service. Their perception of your restaurant is re-adjusted every time they make contact.

Speed of service results from being organized, hustling, and concentrating on doing work quickly. Fast is characterized by moving with ease and quickness, taking a comparatively short time to accomplish work. Fast is often described as prompt, rapid, swift, quick, speedy, timely, and expeditious.

"A lot of restaurants serve good food, but they don't have very good service."

–Wolfgang Puck, celebrity chef.

PRO-ACTIVITY SPEEDS UP SERVICE

To be proactive is to plan ahead, anticipate, and predict events or requests. Proactive customer service involves anticipating a guest's need and fulfilling it before they must ask. Proactive service is meeting and exceeding guests' expectations before they experience a delay or disappointment. A proactive person seldom finds themselves at the mercy of circumstances.

Being proactive means planning out every task and circumstance you will encounter at your restaurant before the need arises. Every system is a mini plan to accomplish a task efficiently, with clear thinking and experience carefully considered.

Proactivity is looking for opportunities to be ahead of the game in pleasing guests and using resources well. Don't be caught unprepared, reacting without planning. Continually apologizing for mistakes and errors is a poor way of doing business that leaves guests unimpressed and frustrated. Proactivity speeds up service and creates higher-quality products. Guest's time in a restaurant for a meal should be determined by them not the restaurant.

Install Systems, Standards, Schedules, and Training That Ensure the Restaurant's Fast Service Standards Are Met

- Food and supplies are being purchased before needed to avoid the time and expense of going to buy them at the last minute.

- Some menu items are being prepared before they are ordered. (Toss salad, pasta cooked, and meats sliced etc.) Care must be exercised to ensure the items being prepared ahead of time maintain their freshness and quality during the holding period. They must be checked for quality if they carry over to the following day.

- Staff members are hired and trained before they are needed to fill schedules.

- Staff members are scheduled so the number of Staff members needed to fulfill Guest's service requirements.

- Guest's seats are pre-selected before they enter the restaurant, so their expectations of being seated immediately are exceeded. For example, Hosts should know where they are going to sit for the next party of 2, 4 and 6 <u>before</u> the Guest arrives.

- Tables are prepared ahead of time, so Guests are seated immediately.

- Below-standard foods are being rejected before a Guest's expectations go unfulfilled.

- Servers are at the table, ready to take a Guest's order before Guests expect service.

- To Go paper and other service items are stocked before it causes Guest service delays.

- Staff members are being cross-trained in other jobs to provide faster Guest service.

- Staff members are moving quickly from place to place and not obstructing the work of others. Hustling gives faster service to Guests while lowering staffing costs.

- Work is being done correctly with a hustle pace.

- Guests are greeted immediately upon entering the restaurant.

- Guests are seated immediately, they are served water, and their orders are taken without delay; their orders are served within a few short minutes; any other needs are met without delay, and they are presented their check as they are finishing their meal.

- Telephones are being answered within three rings and callers are efficiently being helped by a well-trained staff member.

- Opportunities are provided for individual productivity to improve over time continually.

- New staff members carry a full productive workload as soon as possible after being hired.

- Time limits are being set for work completion with the minimum number of staff.

- Staff's personal conversation never interferes with the speed of service.

- Staff member's daily cleaning duties are completed by fitting them in throughout the shift, without interfering with Guest service.

- Equipment needing attention is being maintained before it stops operating correctly.

- Departments are operating at or below their established efficient labor cost standards.

- Opportunities are being sought to speed up service to Guests and other staff members.

- Staff members are trying to astonish the guests with speedy and efficient work while maintaining the restaurant's exacting quality standards.

- Staff members move quickly and never distract or disrupt other staff members' work. Walking six steps per second and stepping a stride of 36 inches without being unsafe to themselves and others.

- Staff members are concentrating on giving Guests their undivided attention.

- Staff members are avoiding distractions and disruptions that slow their production.

- Staff members are avoiding confusion, wasting time, and stopping their work with unnecessary conversation and activities.

- Staff members are using elbow grease to do hand work quickly and carefully. Avoiding wasted motions and duplication of efforts.

- Staff members are eliminating guests waiting for any service. (Seating, ordering, preparing and serving orders, paying.)

- Staff members are planning ahead and using their time wisely during slow periods to prepare for busy periods so they will never find themselves "in the weeds."

- Cooks are preassembling menu items they are sure to be ordered in the next hour.

- Staff members are exhibiting a sense of urgency and maintaining a posture of being ready to respond immediately to any Guest's need.

- Staff members stay on top of service before a rush of Guests to avoid being "in the weeds."

- Staff members never give the appearance that they are relaxed and unprepared to respond immediately with a sense of urgency. They never put their hands in their pockets sit or lean on counters while on duty.

Everyone enjoys prompt service without being rushed.

SIXTH KEY TO $UCCESS
SERVE BEAUTIFUL AND DELICIOUS FOODS

Your Restaurant Must Provide Guests Cuisine that Looks Delightful and Tastes Delicious.

Developing and serving food and beverages that look delightful and taste delicious creates loyalty. Food is the basis of a restaurant, and you must excel in the production and presentation of your food. Average food and beverage quality presents a value problem for your restaurant.

Guests enjoy foods that look delightful and taste delicious. They expect much more than a full stomach. They seek an experience with delicious taste, pleasant service, and visual sensations they cannot get at home. They require hot food to be served hot and cold food to be served cold, with high flavor profiles. People eat with their eyes, and the way food looks and is presented significantly contributes to how it tastes.

Develop Your Food Recipes So They Look Delightful and Taste Delicious. Your foods must taste delicious to your guests, not just you, your chef, your family, or your friends.

Your food types should align with your restaurant's image, name, and style. Develop a sufficient variety to appeal to a broad range of people. Objective sampling and surveying for guest approvals are imperative prior to menu presentation. Consider the flavor profile of popular items today and identify quality foods missing from the marketplace.

Key Considerations

Menu Item Design: Your menu items must be well-designed, presented attractively, and taste delicious and appealing to all your guests. Ask what your target market wants and how they want it when designing menu items.

Quality Ingredients and Preparation: Each recipe should use the best quality ingredients and preparation methods. Establish the ideal variety, storage, preparation methods, style of foods, portion size, and flavor.

Serving Standards: Determine ideal serving temperatures, appearance, presentation, and service style methods.

Taste: Taste includes the flavor profile, bite or chewing texture, sweetness, or tartness. Your food must be uniquely delicious in your market.

Durability and Holding Times: Establish your food's durability and exact holding and storage times for peak serving appearance and flavors. Decide if it can be prepared ahead of time or must be made to order. Ensure it can be prepared within reasonable time constraints and has superior flavor and appearance compared to competitors.

Target Market Alignment

Design your menu items to closely match your target market guest's ideal or perfect product. Research their ideal product preferences. Be objective and set aside personal tastes and pride to ensure every menu item meets guests' expectations of taste and appearance. Iterate through several "ideal" recipes to find the best. Evaluate:

- Is the recipe an improvement on your existing item?

- Is it better than your competitor's comparable item?

- How close is it to your guest's ideal item?

- Can it be produced precisely every time?

- Can it be served quickly to your guests?

- Can it be produced at an acceptable cost?

Ask yourself if guests will "line up around the block" for this item. Sample the product with your "target guest" and ensure they love it.

ONGOING REVIEW AND IMPROVEMENT

Regularly review your menu products. Create a systematic method for testing current products. Monitor sales trends for each menu item. Understand if sales are increasing or decreasing over time. Expanding your offerings to satisfy and delight your guests increases opportunities for differentiating your restaurant from the competition. The opportunity gap lies between what your guests already have and what they really want.

Never, ever cause a Guest the distasteful experience of eating food that is carelessly prepared, bland, poorly seasoned, dried out, over or undercooked, over or under ripe or served at the wrong temperature or consistency.

Documenting And Maintaining Food Quality Processes

Document the food buying, storing, recipe preparation, holding, and serving processes to ensure consistency and accuracy every time. Specify the exact food ingredient brands that make your recipes taste their best. Include detailed recipes in your written systems so they are clear and understood by all staff members. Foods with more flavors generally cost more. Key Areas to Focus On:

- **Equipment and Consistency:** Some variables in a restaurant beverage experience can be due to equipment failure, such as inconsistent carbonation in soft drinks due to valve malfunction or running out of CO2 gas. Following proper portioning or mixing recipes is crucial.

- **Training and Attention:** Poor food quality can stem from a lack of staff training on equipment use or recipes, socializing or daydreaming while working, not setting equipment to proper temperatures, improper thickness settings on slicers, incorrect mixer time or speed settings, and dull slicers and chopping tools.

- **Preparation Timing:** Consistency in cooked or prepared foods can be affected by poor training, inexperience, or lack of attention, such as over or undercooking due to mistaken temperature settings or time variations. Ensure staff follow recipe steps, ingredients, and measurements accurately. Properly drain canned foods and thaw frozen foods to maintain product consistency. Specify exacting food ingredients.

- **Managing Volume:** To handle heavy volume, avoid preparing hot foods too far in advance and storing them under heat lamps, which causes them to dry out and lose texture and flavor. Many products lose appeal quickly, such as fried goods or baked products held overnight. Serve cold foods cold and hot foods hot to maintain quality.

- **Quality Control:** Guests don't understand how a restaurant can serve poor-quality food. This often happens because cooks and management do not taste the items being served. In the rush of preparing many orders, ordinary foods may lose quality. Many guests do not complain, so poor practices go unrecognized.

- **Proper Holding:** Evaporation from soups and sauces held on a steam table can thicken them. Food may lose flavor if not rotated (FIFO) or if thawed improperly. Ensure freshness through proper storage, rotation, and receiving of foods. Address ingredient and measurement errors in food preparation.

- **Ingredient Quality:** Avoid buying lesser-quality foods to minimize costs. Different food brands, varieties, grades, regions, or countries can affect taste and texture. Variations in mixing time can impact flavor. Use the same grade of meat to ensure consistent taste.

- **Food and Beverage Strategy:** Attract guests by serving fresher food that looks delightful and tastes more delicious with improved formulas featuring bright, bold flavors and enhanced savory notes. Every food item must create a delicious flavor event for guests. Continuously improve recipes and preparation methods.

- **Delightful and Delicious Food:** Serve special high-quality food that looks delightful and tastes delicious. Delicious food appeals to guests' senses of sight, taste, chew, and smell, described as delectable, luscious, scrumptious, yummy, and heavenly.

- **Proper Temperature:** Serve and hold food at the correct temperatures to enhance flavors and reduce bacterial growth. Keep hot food above 140°F, cold foods below 40°F, and frozen foods at 0°F.

- People eat with their eyes, so prepare everything to be visually appealing. Foods must consistently look delightful, be well garnished, and have delicious flavors. Food must be attractively placed on plates and in packaging for serving. Foods on display must be fresh and moist without signs of over or undercooking or drying out.

- **Packaging for To-Go Orders:** Determine the best packaging for your food to-go.

Guests may not complain about poor products, but they will not return if their experience is unsatisfactory. A recipe is in chaos when it is distasteful, unattractive, too warm instead of hot, too cool instead of cold, or unavailable.

Ensure food quality to strengthen your restaurant's reputation for providing food that "looks delightful and tastes delicious." Adopt a mindset of continuous improvement: "We haven't made our best menu items yet."

Learning From A Vacation Mishap

Early in my career, I took a rare week-long vacation. I had forgotten to make a particular sauce seasoning spice, and we ran out while I was gone. My staff made the sauce but didn't use any spice in it. Upon returning, I discovered the seasoning spice was gone. When I inquired, the staff said they had used the sauce without any spice. Surprisingly, we didn't receive any known customer comments or complaints about the finished product while I was away. I tasted the sauce and found it noticeably different— bland and unappealing. We had served hundreds of guests an inferior product.

From this experience, I learned two important lessons:

1. The staff will make do when something is missing without much concern.

2. Guests generally do not complain about an unsatisfactory product.

If you think the Guest will tell you if they are unhappy, forget it, they won't. As a restaurant operator, you have the responsibility to protect your guests from product and service mistakes. Guests will assume you have changed your recipe, thinking you certainly couldn't make that kind of mistake.

Elon Musk said, "CEOs should aim to be "absolute perfectionist about the product that you make or the service that is provided," they should also "seek negative feedback from all corners – from customers and from people who aren't customers."

Musk urged business leaders to "take a step back from the situation and ask themselves: "Is our product as awesome at it could be?' Probably not. What could you do to make it great?" The Tesla CEO said, "Companies sometimes think that even though they don't like the product they're making, other people will. "That's not how it works," he said. "If you don't love it, don't expect others will either."

ENSURING ENJOYABLE QUALITY FOOD STANDARDS

- **Attractive Tableware:** The china and glassware are attractive and support the theme of your restaurant.

- **Fresh and Delicious:** Guests perceive the taste and smell of food and beverages as fresh and delicious.

- **Pleasant Texture:** Foods are pleasant to chew with the proper texture, crispness, creaminess, smoothness, and bite.

- **Consistent Quality:** No spoiled, bland, old, or odd flavors are ever perceived by guests.

- **Exact Flavor Balance:** Recipes are rigorously followed to produce the precise flavor balance every time.

- **Proper Serving Temperatures:** Hot foods are best served at 160°F on warm plates, and cold foods are served below 40°F on cool plates.

- **To-Go Packaging:** To-go food packages are neatly folded and closed, with professionally designed packaging displaying the restaurant logo prominently.

- **Guest-Centric Menu:** All menu items are designed with the preferences and ideals of your guests in mind.

- **Systematic Review:** Menu item sales are systematically reviewed to determine their popularity, and efforts are continually made to produce more durable, better-looking, and better-tasting products for guests.

- **Top-Quality Ingredients:** Only top-quality, fresh, ripe foods with delicious flavors are purchased. Do not buy based on price alone, as higher quality foods almost always cost more.

- **Continuous Refinement:** Food recipes and ingredients are continually refined.

- **Proper Food Storage:** All foods are kept covered and sealed to protect them from drying out, contamination by pests, dust, coughs, leaky pipes, and sneezes.

- **Thorough Training:** Staff members are trained to follow clearly written batch recipes every time, ensuring precise portioning, weighing of ingredients, mixing times, cooking and baking times, and temperatures.

- **Quality Checks:** Batches of prepared foods are tasted before storage to ensure the proper recipe is followed and that the resulting product looks delightful and tastes delicious to your guests.

- **Documented Recipes:** All recipes are written and clearly state how to produce final products that look delightful and taste delicious to guests.

- **Exact Preparation:** Cooks prepare all items according to established printed methods and procedures, never skipping steps or abbreviating procedures.

- **FIFO Rotation:** All ingredients and finished products are rotated using the FIFO (first in, first out) method.

- **Safe Handling:** Ready-to-eat foods are safely handled using tongs, spoons, ladles, gloves, scoops, spatulas, pick-up papers, etc.

- **Discard Unsatisfactory Foods:** Foods with expired dates, unusual smells, over or under-ripeness, poor texture, poor consistency, unusual flavor, or appearance are discarded and recorded for reference.

- **Precise Portioning:** Foods are portioned precisely every time to give guests a consistent food experience.

- **Immediate Service:** Freshly cooked menu items are served quickly, as a few minutes in the serving window can change their temperature, appearance, and flavor.

- **Scheduled Oil Replacement:** Cooking oils are replaced on schedule before they pass their prime.

  - **Guest Feedback:** Ask, listen, observe, and ensure that the result of your food quality preparation is that your guests are genuinely enjoying the food they are putting in their mouths.

SEVENTH KEY TO $UCCESS
CREATE ATTRACTIVE AMBIANCE AND DÉCOR

Your Guests Must Enjoy Exciting Visual, Smell, Hearing, and Touch Sensations that Align with the Restaurant Theme.

My experience with décor enhancement was that when done effectively, it increased sales to the point that it was responsible for approximately 30% of our sales.

Creating a restaurant with exceptional décor and ambiance usually requires professional assistance. This is a critical element of your restaurant's presentation. An attractive, inviting, and comfortable environment includes exciting architectural displays, pleasant sounds, and inviting odors. Every aspect, including cleanliness, contributes to the ambiance.

Enhance your restaurant's environment. **Guests expect more than just a table to eat on.** Imagine your restaurant will depend on your décor alone to attract guests. How much enjoyment would your décor have to provide your guests? If your décor package is not interesting enough to admire for a few minutes on its own, then maybe it should be improved. Spend what you need on your décor to make it wonderful because, if done correctly, it will pay for itself in a few months.

Overflow dining rooms are often a diminished, second-class experience with minimal decorating, seating, poor acoustics, or awkward access. Avoid these mistakes to ensure guests have a consistently great experience, even when seated in an overflow area.

Different shapes and colors have different impacts on perceptions. They directly affect our perceptions and can trigger unconscious associations that are positive or negative, gratifying or displeasing. Understanding these differences allows you to communicate more effectively with your guests.

Shapes and colors are among the most direct ways of affecting your guests' unconscious perceptions and influencing their purchasing decisions. Buying decisions are made primarily by the unconscious mind, with the conscious mind justifying the decision. Therefore, like everything else in your sensory package, the shapes and colors you use must be unconsciously compelling.

KEY STRATEGIES FOR CREATING A DELIGHTFUL DINING EXPERIENCE

- **Visual Décor:** Provide an exciting, interesting, and professionally designed visual décor package. Guests require stimulating and pleasant facilities. Provide them with a dining experience in an enjoyable, comfortable environment.

- **Significant Impact of Décor:** Creating an enjoyable décor package can significantly increase sales. Guests are drawn to tastefully decorated facilities with colorful, interesting, and stimulating décor. Although expensive initially, proper décor expenditures can pay for themselves quickly and continue to yield dividends.

- **Reliable Décor:** A well-appointed décor is like the best staff—never late, always on duty, and quietly working to enhance guests' experiences. It only requires regular maintenance and attention to stay intact, clean, and free of tampering.

- **Professional Decoration:** Hire an experienced professional decorator to style your restaurant in line with your desired image. Investing in comprehensive décor rather than skimping on objects, paintings, plants, or other elements will be time and money well spent. Your décor must be more than you and your spouse can put together. Find someone who does interior design for a living to decorate your restaurant. If it truly is a great design, it will work wonders for your restaurant. Don't skimp on this important aspect of your operation.

- **Silent Attraction:** A good décor package attracts guests day in and day out. Extend this décor to the exterior of your building or storefront as well. The more authentic and attractive your restaurant décor, the better.

- **Overall Attractiveness:** Make your restaurant attractive and inviting in every way. Everything your guest sees must be appealing. If your region gets snow, keep sidewalks clear. Keep the entry free of dirt, gum, and litter. Remember, your restaurant's image begins in the parking lot and extends to the landscape, front entryway, lobby, and interior. Guests form an initial impression of your restaurant even before they enter it.

By focusing on these aspects, you can create an inviting atmosphere that enhances the dining experience and encourages guests to return.

INTRODUCTION - DINING BY DESIGN
- EDIE LEE COHEN AND SHERMAN R. EMERY

"What makes a successful restaurant?

One of the designer's major roles in helping to create a successful restaurant is to provide the ambiance – the mood, the atmosphere – those elements which often make the difference between a place merely to "eat out" and one that provides the experience of "dining out." For as most experts agree, people eat out today not just for the food but for the entertainment and for the experience of celebration. Dining out has become a social phenomenon.

It is a combination of factors, then, that leads to a successful restaurant; design, service and food must all work together. More often than not, the successful restaurant is one in which the designer, client and restaurateur have dared to take risks. Not necessarily flamboyant. Just enough risks so that the particular restaurant they've created breaks out of the expected mold. We hope that the projects shown in this book will inspire others to take those risks."

KEEPING YOUR RESTAURANT FRESH AND EXCITING

Time has a way of taking the luster off a restaurant. Eventually, it will get stale if not re-invigorated every few years. There are no steadfast rules about when a restaurant begins losing its edge. What was current five years ago may be outdated today. Nothing can overcome slow service or mediocre food. To keep guests coming, you must excel in all areas by providing enjoyment through great food, fast and friendly service, in a clean and festive atmosphere.

- **Anticipate Decline:** Anticipate that your restaurant sales may eventually decline, and your facilities will need a major facelift with new colors, shapes, and ambiance. No matter how good your concept is, it will become outdated after several years. Renovations and updates are a must.

- **Continuous Adjustments:** Your formulas for success may be great, but they can become an anchor if they prevent you from making continual adjustments. They can hold you in place while the rest of the world keeps moving. A restaurant can easily quickly become outdated with worn finishes, wrong colors and shapes, and an overall tired appearance.

- **Small Changes:** Refresh your restaurant by continually making small changes that guests may only subconsciously notice. Staying steady in today's world is not a cause for celebration. You must keep moving ahead in the restaurant business, or you'll get passed by.

Ensuring Restaurant Quality Décor and Atmosphere Standards Present to Guests a Pleasant Sensory Experience. Guests' sight, hearing, taste, touch, feelings, and smell should all provide a pleasant sensory experience.

By focusing on these aspects, you can keep your restaurant fresh and exciting, ensuring that guests have a consistently great experience every time they visit, even during times when you are packed when overflow seating is required.

Everything in your restaurant must create an enjoyable moment for guests. Your atmosphere and ambiance should include the following elements.

- **Pleasant Sounds:** Protect what your guests hear and ensure they only hear pleasant, enjoyable sounds. Your sensory décor package should surprise and attract guests back by providing background music, not loud foreground music that interferes with their conversations. Avoid causing guests the irritation of hearing instructions to staff members, personal conversations, or loud sounds. Even the sound of dishes clinking may cause discomfort.

- **Private Conversations:** Ensure that guests never hear personal conversations of staff and management's performance evaluations.

- **Comfortable Environment:** Provide guests with comfortable seating and safe walkways with handrails for stairs and inclines.

- **Comfortable Temperatures:** Dining area temperatures should be neutral and carefully monitored, with all air movement indirect and never blowing directly on guests.

- **Visible Décor:** The décor should be clearly visible with good lighting and display presentation.

- **Indirect Lighting:** Use indirect lighting to accent the décor without causing glare or visual discomfort.

- **Inviting Aroma:** The restaurant should smell clean, with whiffs of delicious-smelling foods permeating the space.

- **Clean Facilities:** Guests should never experience décor objects that are soiled, in disrepair, or neglected.

- **Secure Décor:** Décor objects should be attached securely to remain in place and be cleaned regularly.

- **Authentic Theme:** The décor should reinforce the restaurant's theme, giving it an authentic feel.

- **Comfortable Colors and Shapes:** The restaurant's décor colors and shapes should make guests feel relaxed and interested.

- **Interesting Atmosphere:** The atmosphere should be interesting to guests, representing a unique, well-planned, complete, and authentic theme. Your décor should represent a prominent significant aspect of your restaurant.

- **Attention-Grabbing Décor:** Every dining room seat should be surrounded by attention-grabbing décor.

- **Themed Overflow Rooms:** The overflow dining rooms should receive a complete theme décor treatment.

- **Current and Fresh:** The restaurant's theme colors and shapes should be current in popularity and appear fresh.

- **Professional Presentation:** The restaurant's concept and theme should be fully developed into an attractive, professional presentation.

By focusing on these aspects, you can create an inviting and enjoyable atmosphere that enhances the dining experience and encourages guests to return.

"Nobody goes there anymore, it's too crowded."

–Yogi Berra

EIGHTH KEY TO $UCCESS
EXCEED YOUR GUEST'S EXPECTATIONS

Your Restaurant's Guest Experience Must Exceed Their Expectations.

Find those little things in your restaurant operations that provide extra value to your guests, creating a positive and emotionally gratifying experience. You should see joy in their eyes, hear it in their voices, and sense it in their body language. Extraordinary products and services make guests feel pleasure and delight. There are many ways your staff can provide the "Wow Factor" in guest services to delight them and make them want to return.

You must provide your guests with unique value, something they can't get anywhere else, something they value. Otherwise, you'll be in a constant battle to keep your existing guests and find new ones.

A Value Formula - Key Value Ingredients: Prices vs. Enjoyment

Guests require value, a fair deal, in exchange for their time and money. Most people have limited funds to spend and seek to get the most for their money. They require:

- **Fair Prices**

- **Great Service**

- **Delicious Food and portions**

- **Pleasant Décor and Atmosphere**

- **Cleanliness and Sanitation**

Guests are disappointed when their value expectations are not met. They dislike paying for wasteful practices. **Value** is what guests receive for what they pay in money and time. **Net Value** is their enjoyment minus their suffering compared to what they expect.

Guest Enjoyment is a plus for your restaurant's image:

- Orderly experience

- Clean and sanitary facilities

- Prompt seating

- Effective menu presentation and prompt ordering

- Acceptable pricing compared to value received

- Food that looks delightful and tastes delicious

- Order is served correct

- Order is served promptly

- Festive atmosphere and interesting, exciting décor

- Comfortable seating

- Pleasant sights, sounds, and temperatures

- Fast service without delays

- Friendly, attentive staff

- Prompt check presentation

- Sense of order

Guest Suffering is a minus for your restaurant's image:

- Chaotic experience

- Dirty and unsanitary facilities

- Delayed seating

- Slow menu presentation and ordering

- Perceived high prices compared to the value received

- Poor tasting or improperly food temperature

- Ordinary, drab, plain atmosphere and décor.

- Uncomfortable sights, sounds, and temperatures

- Waiting for order delivery

- Wrong order delivered

- Slow guest check presentation

- Indifferent or disengaged staff members

- Sense of chaos

PRICING MENU ITEMS FOR VALUE AND PROFITABILITY

Design your products to be the highest quality possible. Size, portion, and garnish them properly to fit what your target guests want at an acceptable price. Give your guests the best possible product that looks delightful and tastes delicious. Test your finished products with a variety of people, including staff members, selected guests, and yourself, to ensure they are considered excellent by your target market.

Key Steps:

1. **Determine Food Costs:** After designing the best product, calculate the food cost of the menu item. Use computer programs to simplify the task once all ingredients are created and input into the system.

2. **Establish Value for Guests:** Settle on a price that establishes the right value for your guests. Consider what the item will be worth to them in your restaurant. Ensure the item is produced with exact specifications to provide guests with reliably consistent eating experiences every time.

3. **Critical Pricing Process:** Pricing menu items is crucial for successful sales and the restaurant's profitability. Consider the following:

o **Cost-Plus Pricing:** Calculate the total cost of ingredients and multiply by 3, 3.5, or 4 to achieve food costs ranging from 25% to 33% of sales. Add extra costs if there are intense labor costs involved.

o **Competitive Analysis:** Research what your competition charges for similar items. Determine how much you are comfortable charging and what the market (your guests) will accept as a fair price.

o **Consistent Pricing:** Ensure the price is consistent with your other menu items. Consider rounding to the nearest dollar (e.g., $9.00 or 9-), nearest 5¢ (e.g., $8.95), or nearest 9 (e.g., $8.99). Maintain a consistent pricing style theme for all items.

By carefully considering these factors, you can set a price that reflects the value of your menu items while remaining competitive in the market. If you achieve a dynamic décor and efficient, fast, paced service you can add to the menu prices without causing value concerns by your guests.

MENU DESIGN AND ITEM PRESENTATION

Your menu design is a crucial part of your restaurant's image. It communicates your theme, style, and motif. The fonts used, the menu offerings, the ease of reading, and the graphics all together say a lot about your restaurant.

Key Elements of Menu Design:

- **Professional Graphics Designer:** Engage a professional graphics designer to assist with the design elements of your menu.

- **Design Elements:** The paper, size, colors, and graphics all combine to help define your restaurant and its personality or brand.

- **Brand Personality:** Brand personality refers to the personification of the brand. Adjectives like welcoming, comfortable, cool, funny, luxurious, etc., are associated with a brand because of the brand's personality. Each font style has a perception in people's minds. Fonts help reinforce a brand personality as they have their own unique character. Brands can capitalize on this by using the correct type of font for the right content.

- **Consistency:** All design elements of the restaurant must reinforce each other and be consistent with each other. The more consistent the various components of your image are, the stronger your image will be.

Absolutely! The menu is a powerful tool for enticing guests and enhancing their dining experience. Here are some tips on using descriptive adjectives and explaining the unique qualities of your menu items:

CRAFTING MENU DESCRIPTIONS

1. Highlight Key Ingredients:

Use vivid adjectives to describe the main ingredients.

Example: "Fresh, hand-picked organic tomatoes," "succulent, tender filet mignon."

2. Describe Preparation Methods:

Detail how the dish is prepared to add allure.

Example: "Grilled to perfection over an open flame," "slow cooked for hours to enhance flavors."

3. Emphasize Unique Qualities:

Mention any special characteristics that set the dish apart.

Example: "Topped with a zesty lemon-garlic aioli," "served on a bed of aromatic jasmine rice."

4. Create a Sensory Experience:

Engage the senses by describing the aroma, texture, and presentation.

Example: "Aromatic herbs and spices infuse each bite," "crunchy, golden-brown crust with a soft, gooey center."

5. Highlight Provenance and Freshness:

Emphasize the origin and quality of ingredients.

Example: "Locally sourced farm-to-table vegetables," "wild-caught Alaskan salmon."

EXAMPLE MENU DESCRIPTIONS

- **Signature Ribeye Steak:** "Indulge in our succulent, hand-cut ribeye steak, grilled to perfection over an open flame and seasoned with a blend of aromatic spices. Served with a side of our creamy, garlic mashed potatoes and fresh, steamed asparagus."

- **Classic Margherita Pizza:** "Enjoy the simplicity of our classic Margherita pizza, featuring a crispy, wood-fired crust topped with fresh, hand-picked organic tomatoes, creamy mozzarella cheese, and fragrant basil leaves. Drizzled with extra-virgin olive oil."

- **Lemon Herb Grilled Chicken:** "Savor our tender, juicy chicken breast marinated in a zesty lemon-herb marinade and grilled to perfection. Paired with a side of vibrant, sautéed seasonal vegetables and fluffy quinoa."

By incorporating these elements into your menu descriptions, you can create an enticing and memorable dining experience for your guests.

"There is a difference between getting what you pay

for and what you hope for."

–Malcolm Forbes

YOUR RESTAURANT'S KEY PRODUCT ATTRIBUTES

- Provides emotional gratification for guests by satisfying their socialization and hunger needs through the preparation of highly-flavored foods and beverages.

- Offers opportunities to develop and improve family, business, and friendship relationships through conversation, association, and intimacy.

- Provides relaxation, comfort, refreshment, and relief from daily stresses.

- Ensures fast service in a clean, festive, and comfortable atmosphere.

This highlights the importance of functionality in creating a delightful dining experience for your guests, addressing both their emotional and physical needs.

ENSURING YOUR RESTAURANT EXCEEDS VARIOUS STANDARDS AND EXPECTATIONS

Sensory Impact Standards

Food Presentation: Foods look delightful and taste delicious.

- **Cleanliness:** Facilities feel and look clean.

- **Pleasant Smells:** The restaurant smells pleasant.

- **Facility Design:** Shapes are pleasing, communicate warmth, and evoke emotional gratification with therapeutic, rich, and warm colors.

- **Staff Appearance:** Staff members are well-groomed, dressed in clean uniforms, and handle food in a sanitary manner.

- **Comfortable Room Temperatures:** Temperatures are neutral, avoiding any extreme cold or warmth.

Unconscious Association Standards

- **Welcoming Atmosphere:** Guests feel welcome, attracted, and comfortable.

- **Engaged Staff:** Friendly staff engaged with guests, as evidenced by their actions and performance.

- **Clean and Safe:** Clean facilities, sanitary foods, and safe conditions are apparent.

- **Efficient Experience:** Smooth and efficient experience without perceived delays.

- **Attention to Detail:** Great attention to design details and attractiveness of facilities.

- **Privacy for Socializing:** Amenities conducive to guests socializing and conducting business with privacy.

Conscious Mind Conclusions

- **Fast Service:** The service process is fast.

- **Fair Pricing:** The price is perceived as fair.

- **Quality Perception:** Guests think, "It's a busy place; food must be good."

- **Delicious Food:** Food flavors are delicious and served at ideal temperatures.

- **Healthy Appearance:** Fresh food appears delightful and healthy in the right portion.

Packaging Enhancement Examples

- **Branded Products and Services:** Offer branded items like "Friendly, ServFast™ Service," "The Best Salad Bar in Town," "Best Quality Ribs," "Perfect Fruit Pies," "Famous Ranch Dressing," "Fresh Made Pasta," "Old Fashioned Sarsaparilla Soda," "All You Can Eat Buffet," and "Feast for Two" meal packages.

- **To-Go Packaging:** Ensure to-go packaging is appropriate and provides prompt take-out service.

Access and Convenience Standards

- **Responsive Phone Service:** Answer the telephone within two rings.

- **Accessibility:** Ensure the restaurant's dining and to-go parking are easily accessible.

- **Convenient Location:** Locate the restaurant within a convenient driving distance from guests' homes, schools, or offices.

- **Delivery Service:** Provide delivery service.

MAKE YOUR RESTAURANT A ONE-OF-A-KIND "WOW" COMPANY

The objective of your restaurant operations is to exceed the service, product, ambiance, and cleanliness expectations of your guests. This is your opportunity to add value to your restaurant for the price your guests are paying. When you exceed your guests' expectations, you'll achieve two precious things – a loyal, growing base of guests and a hard-to-beat competitive advantage. (A Packed Restaurant.)

Vision and Energy: Dedicate yourself to creating and re-creating the restaurant's vision every day. This vision expresses your hopes and expectations for the future and generates the energy necessary to reach your goals.

Best Management Staff: Hire the best management staff possible and organize them into an efficient working team. Ensure management is thoroughly trained to use the most efficient and best methods in creating enjoyment for guests. Provide ongoing orientation to ensure they have the necessary skills to avoid being over-challenged. Address poor performance individually while recognizing evident progress.

Have Effective Rewards and Values: Embrace change due to the structure of your rewards, values, and beliefs that influence behavior and direct the flow of management energy. Managers should be highly motivated by their successes, with compensation consistent with the results they create.

Provide Access to Information: Make essential information readily available so each manager knows what they need always to take the "Right Action" and can recognize and interpret early signs of trouble.

Interpersonal and Organizational Skills: Teach these skills so management can perform their jobs well. Use self-knowledge and self-management tools to clarify motivations, desires, and personal obstacles. Self-discovery and personal development are as valuable as job knowledge. Managers must be assertive on behalf of their accountabilities and discourage aggressive management styles.

Consistent Values: Ensure the company's culture, "The way we do it here." is strongly composed of values, standards, rules, rituals, and accepted practices. Avoid unseen, hidden, or parallel cultures that send contradictory messages to staff members or guests. Set high standards and do not accept apologies as success. Resolving complaints should be seen as opportunities and a failure to satisfy guests, not just putting out fires.

Full Engagement: Ensure management is fully engaged in an environment where they can use all their skills and abilities to reach higher levels of personal and professional competence.

Enjoy Winning: Have fun winning and meeting each new challenge. A high-performance environment creates a "Game Worth Playing." Guests should value the pleasant experience of doing business with you.

Exceed High Standards: Exceed your guests' high standards every day. Your staff must perform successful behaviors as a habit to participate in your restaurant's success. Convince guests that your restaurant is the best choice for their dining experience.

Understand Guest Preferences: Success in the restaurant business depends mainly on your skill and ability to empathize with your guests. You must have a good feel for their preferences and expectations in a restaurant experience. Develop strong expertise or conduct in-depth market research of your target market's preferences. Knowing what your guests expect and having the skill to provide facilities, services, and products that exceed those expectations is key to beating your competition and winning at the restaurant game.

Ensure Consistent Performance: Your first responsibility is to ensure that your restaurant's performance consistently exceeds the promise you make about your products or services. What wins the loyalty of your guests is exceeding those promises.

- Be a customer in your own restaurant

- Shop your competition

- Survey your guests' experiences

Strive for Perfection: Make every effort to conduct the affairs of your restaurant with great accuracy and precision. Shoot for perfect execution of your systems, knowing that people may not always perform at that level. By stating the objectives, results, and standards in your systems with precision, you will see your products and services executed at a higher level. Your restaurant should be known for high standards by your staff and your guests. The daily operational goal should be to create loyal guests, not just generate sales.

Constantly Improve Value: Keep asking yourself, "What can we do to make our menu items, services, and facilities of greater value to our guests?" Your competition will try to meet their promises, so you'll have the edge if you look at the gaps between your promises and actual delivery. Consistency and reliability count a lot when striving to exceed guests' expectations. By focusing on these aspects, you can create a loyal guest base and beat your competition.

ASTONISHING THE CUSTOMER IS THE KEY TO SUCCESS!

Customer Astonishment: 10 Secrets to World-Class Customer Care. By Darby Checketts

We have entered a new age when mere customer service is not enough. We have entered the age of Customer Astonishment wherein the customer's needs must be more than served - they must be cleverly anticipated. To act before getting asked is the key. Of all the productivity and quality improvement campaigns that will continue to come and go, only one will last, for it is the rediscovery of the most time-honored principle of business success: Find a need and then fill it . . .

#1: Be Customer Champions! Know what your team stands for and communicate it through words and actions. Champion your core purpose in direct response to what your Guests want and need most.

#2: Get Connected. Know the interdependencies represented by your own chain of Guests. Make communication linkage a top priority that demonstrates the importance of all of your Guests, internal and external.

#3: Know Your Guests. Listen to them. Observe them. The commitment is to NO SURPRISES, except on their birthdays. What you promise is what they get and more.

#4: Get It Together. Quickly resolve internal conflicts so these do no become apparent and weaken the customer's confidence in your team. Achieve crystal clear agreement on team priorities and individual responsibilities.

#5: Know the Bear. There is a bear out there behind you. Faster is not fast enough. Reliable is not reliable enough. World Class means you set a standard for the world to follow. The bear cannot keep up.

#6: Take Ownership. Champion the idea that "I am the one." For each member of your team, this means, "I am the one who first spoke with the customer. And, at the end of the day, I am the one who will follow through to be sure WE meet the customer's needs."

#7: Stake Your Reputation. Create your very own Hallmarks of Professional Excellence. Seize those crucial moments of truth in a way that shows your true commitment to each customer.

#8: Add value at Each Step of the Way. Be sure that whatever it is that you do, you do it with the customer in mind.

#9: Smooth the Way. Always treat the customer as an honored guest. Never place your convenience above that of the customer. Your professionalism will shine as you do.

#10: Create Options. Don't say "No" to the customer. NO is often uncreative. YES, it is great, but may be over-commitment. The customer needs options. Create these. Even partial solutions are better than roadblocks. Be a world-class problem solver!

ENSURE YOUR RESTAURANT EXPERIENCE EXCEEDS GUEST EXPECTATIONS

Install facilities, systems, standards, schedules, and training that ensure the restaurant's operating methods and standards exceed your guests' expectations by:

- **Pleasant Appearances:** Ensure your service staff's appearances are more impressive and pleasing to your guests than those at competing restaurants.

- **Friendly and Welcoming Staff:** Have service staff members who smile more, are friendlier, and more welcoming than guests typically experience at competing restaurants.

- **Better Training:** Train your staff better at operating processes than the staff of competing restaurants.

- **Fast Service:** Ensure your service and production processes for delivering food and beverages to guests are faster than they estimated.

- **Responsive Service:** Ensure service staff members respond to unexpected guest service opportunities in a manner that guests find very satisfying.

- **Attractive Food and Beverage:** Present food and beverages that look more delightful to guests than they expect from past experiences and competing restaurants.

- **Delicious Taste:** Ensure the food and beverages taste more delicious than guests usually experience.

- **Well-Designed To-Go Packaging:** Provide to-go packaging that is accommodating to guests.

- **Clean Facilities:** Ensure your restaurant facilities, inside and out, are cleaner than guests expect based on their experiences at competing restaurants.

- **Safe and Sanitary:** Ensure guests perceive your restaurant as safe and sanitary.

- **Comfortable Design:** Ensure your restaurant's design, inside and out, is more comfortable and pleasant than guests' past experiences and competing restaurants.

- **Attractive Ambiance:** Provide a restaurant ambiance and décor package that is more attractive and stimulating than guests' experience at competing restaurants.

- **Pleasant Printed Materials:** Ensure your restaurant's printed information, menus, promotional materials, and signage are perceived by guests as more pleasing and well-done than their expectations.

- **Reasonable Pricing:** Ensure guests perceive your menu pricing as reasonable compared to the value of their total restaurant experience.

- **Consistent Excellence:** Maintain consistently and reliably excellent food, service, and facilities.

By focusing on these aspects, you can ensure that your restaurant exceeds guest expectations and creates a memorable dining experience that encourages them to return.

A guest who has a problem resolved to their satisfaction becomes more loyal than they were previously.

NINTH KEY TO $UCCESS
MAXIMIZE YOUR RESTAURANT'S PROFITABILITY

"No Margin, No Mission"

The saying *"No margin, no mission"* is often used to emphasize the importance of profitability and sustainability. Margin refers to the profit margin or the difference between the cost of producing a good or service and the revenue it generates. Essentially, it's the money left over after all expenses are paid. Mission refers to the goals, purpose, or mission of a restaurant, often related to its core values or long-term objectives.

The phrase implies that without a sufficient profit margin to sustain operations, an organization can't achieve its mission or goals. It's a reminder that financial health is crucial for any business or organization to continue its work and fulfill its purpose. So, the idea is to balance both: ensure that the organization is financially stable (margin) while still staying true to its mission and purpose.

INCREASE PROFIT MANAGEMENT

Always choose guest enjoyment over profit. To achieve a thriving restaurant business, it's crucial to strike a balance between maximizing sales and minimizing costs while ensuring guest enjoyment and satisfaction. Utilize your financial statements to gain insights into and manage your restaurant's performance effectively.

"Your staff members must hustle and be productive for you to succeed. Hustle is profit because it produces faster service, which increases sales while reducing your staffing costs."

Restaurant guests dislike paying for wasteful practices and unproductive staff members standing around. Labor costs will likely be your biggest expense. Profit is the wage of capital and maintains the health of the company. You must drive costs out of the business to ensure profitability and help accomplish staff members' personal goals and your goals.

UNDERSTANDING FINANCIAL STATEMENTS

Income Statement

The income statement shows the profitability of your restaurant over a specific period. It follows the basic equation: **Revenues - Costs = Earnings**. By analyzing this statement, you can determine whether your restaurant earned a profit or incurred a loss during that period.

Balance Sheet

The balance sheet provides a snapshot of your restaurant's financial health at a specific point in time. It follows the formula: **Assets = Liabilities + Owners' Equity**. This statement helps you understand the value and stability of your restaurant.

Key Concepts

- **Assets**: Resources owned by the restaurant, such as money, equipment, and inventory.

- **Liabilities**: Obligations and debts owed by the restaurant.

- **Owners' Equity**: The owners' claim on the assets of the restaurant.

- **Fixed Costs**: Expenses that do not vary with sales, like rent and insurance.

- **Variable Costs**: Expenses that fluctuate with revenues, like food and labor costs.

Importance of an Accountant

A skilled accountant is invaluable to your success as a restaurateur. They help you understand and manage the intricate financial details, ensuring the financial health of your restaurant.

An effective accounting system should:

- Accurately maintain your bank accounts.

- Track the income and expenses of your restaurant.

- Report who you owe money to, how much, and for how long.

- Produce accurate financial statements and reports.

- Generate tax compliance reports.

INCREASE SALES MANAGEMENT

To boost your restaurant's sales, focus on:

- Attracting more guests.

- Increasing the frequency of guest visits.

- Enhancing the average purchase value per guest.

This comprehensive approach ensures a clear understanding of your restaurant's financial health, enabling you to make informed decisions that drive profitability and growth.

Your best strategy for increasing sales is to provide more guest enjoyment thru faster, friendlier services, a cleaner and more sanitary restaurant, better-looking and better-tasting products, and more attractive facilities and décor.

Prioritizing guest experience is key to boosting sales and fostering loyalty. Here are the strategies previously detailed in this book to enhance each aspect of your sales program.

Faster Service

- **Streamline Processes**: *Analyze your service flow and eliminate bottlenecks. Use technology like mobile ordering and payment systems.*

- **Cross-Train Staff**: *Ensure staff can step into different roles when needed, reducing wait times and increasing efficiency.*

- **Optimize Staff Schedules**: *Use historical data to predict busy times and staff accordingly.*

Friendlier Service

- **Training**: *Invest in regular training sessions for staff on customer service skills.*

- **Positive Work Environment**: *Foster a positive work culture to keep staff motivated and happy, which will reflect in their interactions with guests.*

- **Personalized Service**: *Encourage staff to remember regulars and personalize their service.*

Cleaner and More Sanitary Restaurant

- **Cleaning Protocols**: *Implement rigorous cleaning schedules and ensure all your staff adhere to them.*

- **Inspections**: *Regularly inspect all areas of the restaurant to maintain high cleanliness standards.*

- **Hygiene Supplies**: *Ensure all hygiene supplies like hand sanitizers, soaps, and cleaning agents are always stocked.*

Better-Looking and Better-Tasting Products

- **Quality Ingredients**: *Source high-quality ingredients and focus on consistent food preparation.*

- **Presentation**: *Pay attention to food presentation, making dishes visually appealing.*

- **Menu Updates**: *Regularly update the menu to keep it interesting and cater to changing tastes.*

More Attractive Décor Package

- **Interior Design**: *Invest in interior design that aligns with your brand and creates a pleasant dining atmosphere.*

- **Maintenance**: *Regular maintenance of furniture, lighting, and other fixtures to keep everything looking fresh.*

- **Ambiance**: *Use lighting, music, and décor to create a welcoming and enjoyable environment.*

Implementing these strategies can significantly enhance your guests' experience, encouraging repeat visits and creating positive word-of-mouth recommendations.

The most critical times when your staff executes your battle plans and tactics are during the breakfast, lunch, and dinner periods when the majority of sales occur. Your staff needs all the assistance and support they can get from you and their managers or supervisors. Hiring, interviewing, scheduling your staff, holding management meetings, and training are important but must be done before and after these busy periods. Management should be on the floor assisting your staff, ensuring they are doing their work correctly and quickly.

You can learn about guests' preferences through surveys, interviews, server feedback, guest comment cards, and online survey responses. You can increase your guests' average purchases by promoting items with higher prices and effectively promoting add-on items such as side orders and desserts. This can be accomplished with more effective menu presentation and more effective sales suggestions from your staff. You should keep 100% of all promises to guests.

Make guests come alive by displaying letters and notes from them for your staff members. You can make quality guest service and reliability an obsession with your staff members by recounting "success stories" about how staff members served guests well.

Never accept a year-over-year sales decrease without discovering the reasons. Occasionally, a change in the economy or market conditions can influence sales. Don't look for excuses for sales declines with competition or the economy. This is a very dangerous and slippery slope. One can always find excuses for weak sales by blaming competition or market conditions.

A decrease in sales usually indicates a weak operation that is not providing guests with a better experience. It can also be a major theft occurring in the restaurant. There could be circumstances where a restaurant is dependent upon a single industry or economic force. If you are in a tough market, you must work harder and do a better job. If you are in a great market, so much the better. Find ways to deal with the poor market or move your restaurant. Every day, you can make improvements for guests. You have a year to make enough improvements with food, service, facilities, and cleanliness to cause sales to improve next year.

The life cycle of all businesses follows a bell curve. There is the beginning stage when the business begins operations. The growth stage follows this stage, then the maturity stage, and finally the decline stage. Your objective is to extend the life of your business to fifty years or more, if possible. The important thing is to always, always stay in the growth stage. This is critical to any business's long-term success. Never take sales declines lightly or give in to excuses like the competition is getting stronger or the economy is getting weak. Every time our sales increase faltered or declined, we got agitated and figured out a better course of action that could take us back to the growth stage. Over 50 years, I never felt like the economy was the major factor in our sales increases or decreases. I found our sales results were more related to our execution of the project to serve guests better.

THE SLAYMAKER CASE STUDY ON PROMOTION VS. ATTRACTION

To illustrate my point about promotion versus attraction, I'll relay what Don Morehouse, a friend and the president of the local Slaymaker Group, told me about their advertising program. In the 1990s, Slaymaker Group had national franchises for TGI Fridays, Tony Roma's Ribs, and Wingers Grill and Bar. Don told me they had an ongoing television advertising program for their group of franchise brands. Each month, they would feature one restaurant brand in their group. They would rotate through each brand over three months. Each month, the restaurants being featured on TV would see an increase in sales while they were on television. When the restaurant brand was due for advertising three months later, the sales for that brand would be back to the level they were before the advertising began. That told me that they were not providing enough value and enjoyment for their guests to keep them coming without the advertising. They eventually closed Tony Roma's Ribs and TGI Friday's.

'There are many ways to lose your shirt in the restaurant business, but only one way to succeed . . . . Keep your eye on everything."

–Karl Karcher, Carls Jr. Restaurants

CREATE POSITIVE WORD OF MOUTH ADVERTISING

Guests often share their restaurant experiences with others. Those who feel their negative experience was not satisfactorily resolved typically tell an average of eleven people and tend not to return. In contrast, a satisfied guest tells an average of five people. The cost of service and product errors is difficult to determine. If one guest visits a restaurant every three weeks and spends $25 on each visit, the cost of losing them is $435 per year. If that person influences eleven other people to avoid your restaurant, you could lose nearly $4800 per year. A dissatisfied guest may never return, and a loyal guest's future patronage is far more valuable than their current spending.

If there is a possibility of guest dissatisfaction, encourage complaints or comments. Your reaction to feedback is crucial, as it promotes repeat business. Treat guests in a way that turns them into loyal customers who return often.

Implement Shadow Coaching Management Systems, Quality Review Inspections, and management-orchestrated friendly hospitality dining systems to ensure a high-quality guest experience. This strategy requires a high-caliber management staff to execute. It guarantees that every guest's experience aligns with your vision and systems. Positive word of mouth is the most believable form of promotional communication and cultivates extremely loyal guests.

Your purpose should be to create a positive enjoyment image in the minds of guests, attracting them back to the restaurant often by delivering flavor, beauty, cleanliness, friendliness, and comfort." Seek favorable publicity by participating in community fundraising events and supporting community development activities and organizations.

Media Advertising

Your media advertising goal should be to minimize paid advertising and rely on operational effectiveness to yield better results with greater effort, providing real value for guests. Ensure you have an effective internet presence and a well-designed website.

Marketing Strategy

Your primary marketing strategy should focus on "Setting the Course for Customer Satisfaction." Your systems should aim to create loyal guests who will return often. If the traditional family is your primary target market, consider that the mother is often the primary decision-maker in choosing where the family dines. She will select the restaurant that brings the most enjoyment to her family. She seeks a dining experience where family relationships can be strengthened and interactions can occur in a positive atmosphere without the distractions of poor cleanliness, poor staff member appearance, slow service, order mistakes, or poor-quality food.

She seeks satisfaction through enjoyable personal interactions with her family and restaurant staff, comfortable and well-decorated facilities, and full value for her money. Her requirements include reliability and proven quality in the cleanliness and maintenance of facilities, the nutrition, appearance, and taste of food, and the clean appearance, friendliness, and attentive service of the staff.

When you do advertise in the media, ensure that your advertising pieces are professionally designed with high artistic quality compatible with your restaurant's image. The typeface, color, feel of the presentation, layout, and writing tone should all create a unified image of the restaurant that aligns with every other element of your restaurant's facilities, menus, printed materials, letterheads, packaging, and company logo.

System-Driven Business

Your restaurant should be a system-driven business where every system is designed as part of your marketing strategy.

"When you can shift your inner awareness to how you can serve others, and when you make this the central focus of your life, you will then be able to know true miracles in your progress toward prosperity."

–Wayne W. Dyer, motivational speaker

Competing in Your Trading Area

Competing in the marketplace is like a chess match, but it's not your usual game of chess. It's a game in which you invent your own pieces and moves. You'd think that would give you an insurmountable advantage, but the other players are doing the same thing. This creates a challenging, freewheeling game filled with fun and satisfaction. To win the restaurant battle, you must out-organize, out-clean, out-friendly, out-decorate, out-hustle, and out-delicious your competition.

You need to study your competition to understand their strengths and weaknesses. Then, study your trading area to identify the products and services that your potential guests desire. You must know what your restaurant needs to provide to be superior to your competition and please your guests.

Make "positive word-of-mouth publicity" the backbone of your marketing strategy.

"We're Glad You're Here" Marketing Strategy Standards

- **Comprehensive Training:** Ensure thorough and ongoing training that makes your systems well-understood and consistently practiced by your staff.

- **Shadow Coaching:** This is the final step in the training process, ensuring that your marketing strategy systems are effectively implemented.

- **Quality Management and Orientation:** Provide guests with quality management and continual staff orientation to maintain high standards.

- **Positive Attitudes and Behaviors:** Staff members should exhibit positive attitudes and behaviors at all times.

- **Friendly Interaction:** Staff members should interact with guests in a friendly and personable manner.

- **Full Attention to Guests:** Ensure every staff member gives full attention to the guests they interact with.

- **Respectful and Helpful Attitude:** Staff should communicate a respectful, helpful attitude through the care of your facilities, their appearance, and how they prepare and serve food.

- **Prompt and Quality Service:** Products should be carefully prepared and delivered to guests without delay.

- **Creating Enjoyment:** Build an enjoyment image in guests' minds that attracts them back by delivering flavor, beauty, cleanliness, friendliness, and comfort.

- **Loyal Guests:** Cultivate loyal guests who return often due to the enjoyment they previously experienced through your "We're Glad You're Here" strategy.

- **Effective Operating Systems:** Implement highly effective operating systems that provide real value to your guests.

- **Value Pricing:** Offer value pricing for lunch and late-night guests.

- **Word of Mouth Promotion:** Leverage word of mouth as the backbone of your promotional strategy, as it is the most believable form of advertising.

- **Enjoyable Experience:** Focus on creating an enjoyable experience for guests so they speak positively about your restaurant and recommend it to others.

- **Attractive Menus:** Ensure your menus are attractive, interesting, easy to read and understand, and promote your most profitable items.

"Beware of little expenses; a small leak will sink a great ship."

–Benjamin Franklin

DECREASE COSTS MANAGEMENT

Never choose cost control over guest enjoyment.

Adopt a 28-Day Accounting System

A 28-day accounting system makes it easy to compare sales and expenses period by period thirteen times per year. The 12-month accounting system makes it difficult to make comparisons because of the varying number of weekend days in a month. They are typically higher sales days. Payroll is typically every two weeks, making two pay periods in every accounting period.

To effectively control costs, you need a robust accounting system to track expenses and promptly identify rising costs. An effective accounting system requires accurate sales information, expense details, and inventory data.

Expense Tracking: Ensure all invoices and charge slips are entered into the accounting system. Keep them secure until they are processed in your accounting office. Every purchase should be documented with an invoice signed by an authorized person. Misplaced invoices can lead to misinformation on profit and loss statements and delayed payments.

Sales Computation: Use a reliable method to account for sales and match revenue with actual bank deposits. Given that credit card sales are predominant, negotiate with multiple processors to get the best discount rates. Have a secure method for depositing cash and checks directly into your bank. Ensure all sales data matches your deposited revenue by the end of each month.

Year-over-Year Sales Comparison: Comparing sales year-over-year helps determine if your restaurant is growing. It's your ultimate scorecard for assessing the effectiveness of your guest-friendly systems. To compare sales accurately, match similar periods. For instance, different numbers of weekends in April across various years can distort your sales comparison. With a 28-day accounting system, you have 13 equal accounting periods annually, providing more frequent monitoring and one extra profitability report. This system ensures accurate sales forecasts and staffing schedules, enhancing service quality.

Systematic Inventory Counting: Adopting a 28-day accounting period means inventory days will always fall on the same day of the week, making counting more systematic and convenient. Your accountant can easily reconcile your monthly accounts payable and bank statements with this system.

CONTROL COSTS OF DOING BUSINESS

Your systems should aim to create loyal guests who return with the lowest cost. Your strategy should focus on operating with lower costs while providing guests with cleaner facilities, faster and friendlier service, and more delicious food without compromising the guest experience.

- **Efficient Labor and Food Use:** Use labor efficiently and follow recipes to avoid food wastage. Avoid wasting supplies, water, sewer, natural gas, and electricity.

- **Controlling Variable Costs:** This is essential to earning a profit and ensuring the restaurant's continued existence. Working at a hustle pace helps reduce labor costs.

- **Pricing Strategy:** The last option to lower food costs is to increase the price of some or all menu items. Increasing the price of best sellers will have the most impact on food costs but may turn off guests. If guests notice the price increase and resist buying, the decision may have been poor. One adage is that increasing prices by 1% decreases the number of guests by 1%. Being underpriced leaves profit on the table, while being overpriced does not maximize guest counts. The average profitable restaurant has prime costs (food & beverage, To-Go packaging, and labor) that amount to 60% of sales.

- Your strategy should never cut costs at the expense of the guest's enjoyment experience. Instead, focus on providing real value to guests through effective cost-control measures.

CONTROL FOOD USAGE SYSTEM

The objective of controlling food costs is to ensure the correct amount of food is used in recipes to minimize costs while providing full value to guests. Calculate your ideal food costs with a computer program that uses the precise amount of product for each menu item. The sales mix of your menu items determines your food cost percentage of sales for a given period. Compare the ideal cost of food against the actual cost to determine your restaurant's actual operating shrinkage in dollars. Identify the causes of shrinkage, which may include:

- **Unreported Sales:** Theft of cash collected from guests.

- **Unauthorized Giveaways:** Food and beverages are given away without being charged (either by mistake or intentionally).

- **Staff Consumption:** Employees eat food or beverages without recording or paying for them.

- **Complimentary Meals:** Meals being given away or stolen by guests.

- **Over-portioning or Waste:** Over-cooking, over-trimming, or excessive portion sizes.

- **Purchasing Discrepancies:** Charges for food and beverages not received or no credit for returns.

- **Price Fluctuations:** Changes in the price paid for food and beverages.

By addressing these issues, you can better manage food costs and improve your restaurant's profitability.

The Overall Solution to High Food Costs Is More Active Supervision, Better Systems of Spot Checks – And Prioritized Duties. When Problems Develop, Fix the Biggest Problems First.

EFFECTIVELY PURCHASE HIGH-QUALITY FOOD AND SUPPLIES AT THE LOWEST PRICE

Effective purchasing is a crucial first step in controlling the cost of goods for your restaurant. Buying food can be akin to buying a car; typically, food salespeople are paid based on their sales volume and profit margin, charging what the market will bear. Prices can vary significantly between different restaurants on a sales route, with salespeople having discretion over pricing. Larger restaurants generally receive better pricing, while smaller ones may pay more. Never purchase food items without comparing prices between at least two competing vendors. A good computer inventory program is essential for tracking and comparing vendor prices.

- **Efficient Sales Management:** Limit sales visits to one day a week, keeping interactions brief and focused on business. Cultivate a cooperative relationship with salespeople while respecting their and your time.

- **Objective of Effective Purchasing:** Ensure the continual availability of specified quality materials at the best price. Use purchase orders to maintain proper receiving and plan for items that may be in short supply or difficult to procure.

- **Vendor Selection:** Determine the vendor with the lowest price for products meeting your specifications—carefully screen product specifications, as variations can affect taste, yield, and appearance. Communicate orders in person, telephone, or fax.

- **Purchasing Standards:**

o Prioritize quality, flavor, durability, and taste over price when purchasing materials.

o Avoid undue influence of friendship or sentimental motives; do not accept gifts from vendors.

o Aim for every possible savings and product improvement, considering material consistencies, flavors, textures, warranties, and service.

o Obtain bids from at least two vendors for major items and choose the lowest-price vendor with equal service and availability.

- **Vendor Price Quote Process:**

o Determine exact specifications for high-quality flavors.

o Provide vendors with a "Vendor Price Quote Sheet" and bidding instructions.

o Encourage vendors to submit bids only on items meeting your exact specifications.

o Reject quotes for items that do not meet specifications.

o   Ensure price adjustments for pack size differences are noted.

o   Require vendors to submit guaranteed price quotes for at least one month and update vendor price lists monthly.

o   Obtain material price quotes in numerical order for consistency.

o   Allow substitute brands only with permission and sample approval.

o   Expect vendor prices to be stable for at least one month, requiring a minimum 1% price reduction from the current vendor to qualify as the lowest bid.

- **Bulk Purchases:** Make large quantity purchases to reduce costs while maintaining high-quality standards. If you have sufficient storage space you can benefit from bulk purchases while negotiating better prices with volume purchases. Order up to par levels for savings under 2% of the current lowest price and opt for volume purchases for non-perishable items when savings exceed 2%.

"One boy--whole boy; Two boy--half boy; Three boy--no boy."

– One person working alone can do the work of two distracted persons, and many people together can be distracted by each other such that they don't accomplish any work.

EFFECTIVELY CONTROL YOUR LABOR COSTS

The objective of labor cost control is to:

1.   Ensure accurate payment for time worked by staff members.

2.   Provide excellent guest service.

3.   Manage labor costs to minimize expenses and maximize guest satisfaction.

- **Shift Labor Accountability Report:** Develop a report that includes the current average wage rate and a fair standard labor cost percentage for the department to achieve excellent service results. Allow enough labor hours to provide good service without wasting resources.

- **Monitor Time Worked:** Review the time worked by all department staff members at the close of each shift. Ensure that all recorded work times are accurate. Avoid buddy punching (when one staff member signs in and out for a friend). Resolve any questions about the accuracy of time worked before the end of the day.

- **Calculate Total Costs:** Multiply the hours worked by the average rate to determine the total labor costs as a percentage of sales for each shift.

- **Compare Standard Costs:** Compare the actual labor costs to the standard costs to determine the over or underuse of labor for the shift. Aim to operate each shift at or below the restaurant's labor cost standards.

- **Manager Accountability:** Establish each manager's total over/under operating percentage amount for a period of weeks or months to track performance.

"Productivity is being able to do things that you were never able to do before."

–Franz Kafka, German novelist

INCREASE YOUR STAFF MEMBERS' PRODUCTIVITY

The effective use of labor is essential for providing an experience that keeps guests coming back. Although labor is often the single greatest operating cost, it should not dictate the level of service. A properly trained and managed staff should operate within your established labor standards. By managing labor effectively, you can achieve high staff productivity and deliver fast, complete service.

- **Labor Cost and Productivity:** Labor costs are the result of the time it takes your staff to perform their tasks. It's crucial to maintain the correct ratio of staff to service, production, and cleaning every shift. When you don't meet your labor standards, your staff members may not perform to their potential. Guests dislike seeing unproductive staff members, and an unproductive staff is costly.

- **Measuring Labor Productivity:** Labor productivity measures the average hustle generated by staff members during the shift. *Work tends to expand to fill the time allotted for its completion.* The more time you schedule for work, the higher your labor costs will be if it doesn't result in the appropriate level of sales.

- **Improving Productivity:** Each staff member's productivity naturally improves with practice. Managers must assist them in reaching their true productivity potential by consistently allotting less and less time to complete tasks until they achieve their highest reasonable productivity capacity. Like a rubber band, they stretch and stretch until they reach their maximum length (productivity). However, never stretch a person beyond their breaking point or until they cannot perform their work correctly.

You can minimize costs by effectively managing labor and fostering a productive work environment while maximizing guest satisfaction and staff efficiency.

The secret to motivating is to provide the consequences of rewards for valuable behavior and penalties for misbehavior. A person's mind operates by two principles: The principle of profit of action and/or the principle of least effort.

ACHIEVE A FAIR LABOR STANDARD

To ensure staff member productivity aligns with your established labor cost standard. It provides excellent guest service, management must take the lead in assisting staff members to increase their work pace.

- **Staff Scheduling:** Begin each shift with the correct number of staff members scheduled to achieve labor costs and quality service according to sales projections. Avoid over-scheduling staff.

- **Preparation During Slow Periods:** Use slow periods to prepare for busy times by stocking up on food and supplies, cleaning, and more.

- **Develop Weak Skills:** Move staff members to their weakest workstations during slow periods to develop their productivity.

- **Cross-Training:** Build a strong team by cross-training staff members in different jobs. This allows for rotation, providing fast service and variety in their work. This flexibility enables effective shift management with fewer staff members. All staff members should be equally busy throughout a shift.

- **Keep Staff Busy:** Keep staff members busy and challenged with a full workload by adjusting work assignments, moving them between workstations, having them clean, giving breaks, or sending them home. Remember, *"If there is time to learn, there is time to clean."*

- **Accurate Pay:** Ensure staff members are paid for their actual time worked by checking their in, out, and meal break times making corrections as needed.

- **Productivity Pace:** Staff members are productive if they are walking 6 feet per second and performing handwork quickly. They should work at their capacity pace.

- **Coaching:** Coach individual staff members to improve their work speed. Work side by side with them to illustrate standard productivity expectations.

- **Set Time Limits:** Set time limits for tasks to be completed, such as closing and cleaning work, preparing orders, counting down tills, and stocking foods.

- **Cleaning During Shifts:** Have staff perform cleaning tasks during the shift to minimize end-of-shift cleanup time.

- **Performance Standards:** Each individual staff member should be performing work at or above your minimum fair labor standard pace.

By implementing these strategies, you can ensure your restaurant performs effectively at or below your established labor cost standard while maintaining high levels of guest satisfaction.

"The key to successful leadership today is influence, not authority."

–Ken Blanchard, motivational speaker, author

MAKE AN EFFICIENT LAYOUT FOR PEOPLE TO WORK

When designing a restaurant layout and planning workspaces, it is crucial to consider the proximity of equipment, tables, and storage areas. Efficient layouts minimize steps and reaching, thereby reducing wasted time and energy, which is critical for an effective restaurant operation.

- **Minimize Movement:** Position equipment, tables, and storage areas close to each other to avoid unnecessary movement. Aim to create a workflow that allows staff to complete tasks with minimal steps.

- **Wide Aisles and Room to Move:** Ensure there are wide aisles and ample space for staff to move around the restaurant comfortably.

- **Reduce Obstacles:** Minimize stairs and other obstacles to create a smooth and efficient flow of movement.

- **Efficiency Focus:** The key is to design layouts that minimize steps and movement, enabling staff to work efficiently.

"What's measured improves" and *"Management is doing things right; leadership is doing the right things."*

–Peter F. Drucker

TIME AND MOTION STUDY

A time and motion study involves direct and continuous observation of tasks using a timekeeping device (e.g., stopwatch or videotape camera) to record the time taken to accomplish tasks with repetitive work cycles. This study helps identify areas where efficiency can be improved and processes streamlined.

"A time and motion study is a business efficiency technique combining the Time Study work of Frederick Winslow Taylor with the Motion Study work of Frank and Lillian Gilbreth. It is a major part of scientific management. After its first introduction, time study developed in the direction of establishing standard times, while motion study

evolved into a technique for improving work methods. The two techniques became integrated and refined into a widely accepted method applicable to the improvement and upgrading of work systems. This integrated approach to work system improvement is known as methods engineering and it is applied today to industrial as well as service organizations, including banks, schools and hospitals."

–Wikipedia

Equipment Updates and Investment

Equipment manufacturers are continuously improving the tools available to the food service industry. Staying up-to-date with the latest equipment can reduce costs and enhance product quality. Equipment is expensive and specific to each type of restaurant. Once purchased, it depreciates in value and must be heavily utilized to pay for itself before being retired over time.

Controllable Expenses

Controllable expenses in a restaurant include theft and embezzlement, advertising and marketing, equipment repairs, and utilities such as electricity, natural gas, water, and sewer. Technology costs should also be monitored. For the average restaurant, these expenses should amount to no more than 20% of sales.

Control Utility Costs

The objective of utility cost control is to minimize energy waste without decreasing guest satisfaction or operating efficiencies. Implementing energy-saving practices and using efficient equipment can help achieve this goal.

Control Electricity Costs

- **Turn Off Lights:** Turn off lights in unoccupied rooms. Lights generate heat, which burdens cooling systems in summer and is an expensive way to heat in winter.

- **Manage Outdoor Lighting:** Turn off outside building and signage lights 5 minutes after closing time and parking lights one hour after closing time. Ensure outside lights are not coming on during the daytime due to a faulty timer setting.

- **HVAC Management:** Avoid overheating or overcooling rooms with HVAC systems. Keep dining room temperatures comfortable for guests. Staff might prefer different temperatures suited to their working conditions, which might not be comfortable for seated guests. It's not uncommon for dining rooms to be too cool for some guests.

Control Natural Gas Costs

- **Turn Off Unused Equipment:** Turn off ovens, cookers, warmers, and grills when they are not in use to save energy.

- **Adjust Cooking Flame:** Ensure the cooking flame on gas-fired units is adjusted to be entirely blue with a firm center cone. A yellow-orange tip indicates that some gas is not being burned, and the flame should be turned down.

- **Maintain Simmering Heat:** Turn down the heat as soon as food begins to boil to maintain liquids at a simmer. Water and other water-based liquids boil at 212°F. Turning the burners higher will not cook food faster. It only uses more energy.

- **Set Thermostats Appropriately:** Set equipment thermostats to the established temperature to achieve the desired results efficiently.

- **Optimize Oven Use:** Load ovens to capacity to utilize as much cooking heat as possible. Load deck ovens quickly to minimize heat loss and avoid opening oven doors frequently, as each second the door is open drops the interior temperature by 10°F.

- **Water Heater Settings:** Set water heaters to 140°F and dishwasher booster heaters to 180°F for optimal energy use.

Control Water and Sewer Costs

- **Minimize Water Use:** Ensure that water and sewer costs are minimized. Every time water is used, some is wasted. Sewer costs are higher than water in most areas and are based on the amount of water used. Take care of our environment and natural resources.

- **Efficient Dishwasher Use:** Fill the dishwasher to fully utilize electricity, hot water, detergent, and rinse aid.

- **Use Hot Water Efficiently:** Use hot water for cooking and filling steam tables. A water heater uses less energy than a steam table to heat the same amount of water.

- **Avoid Unnecessary Water Use:** Never allow water to run unnecessarily. Ensure water faucets shut off thoroughly after use. Small drips can cost big money.

Control Theft and Embezzlement - Maintain an Honest Working Environment

As a restaurant operator, you are responsible for ensuring the honesty of your staff members. Establish controls to safeguard cash and other valuables, making it difficult for staff members to commit theft. Utilize security cameras to help maintain an honest environment. Dishonesty is a continual threat to the financial security of every restaurant.

- **Supervision and Systems:** Provide close supervision and implement sound operating systems to minimize temptations for staff members working around food, beverages, supplies, tools, credit cards, and cash. If one staff member is dishonest, others may follow. As the saying goes, "One bad apple spoils the barrel." Almost anyone can succumb to the temptation of theft and dishonesty if given the right conditions.

- **Zero Tolerance Policy:** There should be no second chance for theft in your restaurant. People who steal always rationalize their behavior. Eliminate dishonesty when you find it to prevent it from spreading throughout the company. Poor morale is often associated with dishonest conditions.

By maintaining an honest working environment, you can protect your restaurant's financial security and foster a positive atmosphere for both staff and guests.

One study of restaurant staff members found some 62% admitted to stealing cash or property. The study also found that 53% admitted watching others steal and not reporting it. 78% owned up to various forms of "company time theft." 80% of staff members surveyed admitted to counter-productive behavior, such as damaging property while horsing around, purposely wasting company materials, consuming drugs or alcohol while on the job and doing sloppy work while hung over from drugs or alcohol.

Another study found that entry-level staff members in the restaurant industry admitted having stolen an average of $254 per year (cash and merchandise) from their employers. Staff member theft has a strong impact on the restaurant industry. According to the United States Chamber of Commerce, annual revenue loss due to staff member theft contributes to approximately fifty percent of small business failures within the first year (Oliphant & Oliphant, 2001).

Costs of staff member theft in the restaurant industry are estimated at $4 to $7 billion (Garber & Walkup, 2004*).*

Typically, staff member theft in food service falls into two categories: "shrinkage" the loss of inventory or "larceny" the loss of cash or merchandise. Food and liquor inventory, unpaid food consumption, credit card fraud, stolen tips, giving unauthorized discounts, and free food given to friends or family are just a few examples of staff member theft in the restaurant industry. Moreover, these types of theft may often go undetected for long periods of time because proper internal control procedures are not in place (Garber & Walkup, 2004).

THEFT AND EMBEZZLEMENT SITUATIONS

Staff member dishonest behaviors include:

- Taking money from their till and quitting.

- Using the manager code to return items on guest checks and pocketing the difference.

- Taking food out the back door.

- Placing food in the outside dumpster for later retrieval.

- Giving food to friends or family for favors.

- Trading food with friends at other businesses.

- Voiding guest checks after collecting cash from guests and keeping the cash.

- Unauthorized eating of food or pocketing candy or individual food items.

- Adding additional charges to customer credit card purchases and then quitting their job, leaving the restaurant with a shortage when the customer reports the overcharge.

- Allowing guests to feed others with all-you-can-eat buffet items.

- Allowing guests to walk out without paying for meals served.

The acceptance of theft is so widespread that, according to one study. At the same time, 7% of respondents admitted to taking between $10 and $100 a week, and 52% believed the "average" staff member pocketed between $10 and $200 per week.\

Steps to Creating an Honest Working Environment That Reduces Pilferage and Theft

- **Be Aware of and Watch for Dishonest Practices:** Do not overlook dishonest actions, such as food carried out at the back entrance, breaking food taken out, serving friends free food, asking for larger portions, and serving larger portions.

- **Reinforce Honesty Requirements:** Remind staff members about the restaurant's honesty requirements during performance reviews. Employment must be based on honesty and willingness to disclose dishonest acts of others.

- **Monitor Temptation Points:** Closely monitor conditions where people are tempted, especially those with access to money, credit card information, food, or supplies.

- **Secure Product Storage:** Guard against theft of products by securing storage rooms with locks and security cameras.

- **Guard Against Cash Theft:** Establish cashier standards of one person per till. Implement accurate cash-out procedures and monthly recaps of individual over/under results. If all cost accounts have increased and sales levels are normal, it strongly suggests cash theft.

- **Secure Bank Deposits:** Establish a secure bank deposit system to safeguard cash.

- **Minimize Self-Serving:** Minimize staff preparing or serving their food or that of friends and family. Avoid over-portioning break meals.

- **Prevent Food Giveaways:** Guard against staff members giving away food to friends and family. Every menu item must be recorded and priced before it is prepared.

- **Lock Valuables:** Keep gates, doors, cabinets, safes, or offices with valuables locked.

- **Use Security Cameras:** Install security cameras to monitor vulnerable dishonest acts.

- **Limit Access:** Limit unoccupied restaurant access without a security system alarm set.

- **Protect Keys and Pass Codes:** Do not lend keys to anyone or share computer passcodes.

- **Monitor Staff Departures:** Be aware of staff members leaving the restaurant to ensure they do not have concealed restaurant property. Inspect jackets and backpacks when theft is suspected.

- **Accompany Visitors:** Accompany vendors, truck drivers, and off-duty staff members to storage areas.

- **Confront Dishonesty:** Address the taking of restaurant cash, tools, food, supplies, and other property, as well as giving away food/beverages or taking cash from the cash drawer.

- **Act Promptly:** Act promptly to eliminate dishonesty. Terminate staff members for dishonest acts. Never give a second chance for theft, as soft management breeds dishonesty.

- **Public Accountability:** Make it known within the organization that there has been a termination due to theft. Public accountability gives others good reason to avoid similar behavior.

"Most people who fail in life is not because they aimed too high, but because they aimed too low and hit."

–Les Brown

Install Systems, Standards, Schedules, and Training That Ensure Your Restaurant's Cost Control Systems Are Performed Properly

- **Accounting System:** Install a comprehensive accounting system that tracks your revenues and costs by department, comparing current data against year-to-date and previous years' data. This helps you understand how your revenues, expenses, and net income are trending.

- **Money Handling:** Always involve two people in counting and depositing money to maintain accountability.

- **Document Control Systems:** Document your restaurant control systems in writing for consistency and clarity.

- **Accurate Food Production:** Plan accurate food production to avoid overproducing perishable items minimizing waste through spoilage.

- **Exact Portioning:** Implement systems for exact portioning of foods using scales, ladles, scoops, or other measuring devices.

- **Prevent Food Theft:** Prohibit food theft by monitoring grazing and snacking of staff members.

- **Avoid Accounting Errors:** Take simple but accurate food and supply inventories, base accurate costs on usage rather than purchases, accurately account for paid outs/coupons and overrings, account for all guest checks, and keep precise food dump sheets.

- **Regular Inventory:** Take inventory at least monthly or more frequently if shrinkage is unsatisfactory. Consider weekly or daily inventories for more costly products.

- **Product Specification:** Specify exact products to avoid using the wrong items. Strengthen purchasing and receiving procedures.

- **Identify Shrinkage:** Determine if food shrinkage is due to staff consumption.

- **Minimize Food Waste:** Ensure good food is not wasted or discarded unnecessarily. Evaluate suspected spoilage or contamination to determine if food is still usable. Staff may be quick to discard food, so assess color, texture, thickness, and consistency.

- **Correct Spoilage Causes:** Identify and correct the causes of food spoilage.

- **Record Food Waste:** Document all food waste on a food waste report for management evaluation. Assess reasons for waste, such as dropping, burning, spoiling, overcooking, or over-trimming.

- **Prevent Order Remakes:** Ensure servers and order takers clarify orders with guests to avoid misunderstandings. Ensure cooks read orders correctly with clearly printed instructions.

- **Inspect Empty Containers:** Regularly check empty cans and containers to ensure all food is used.

- **Conduct Trash Audits:** Periodically perform trash audits to discover excessive waste. Dump out full trash cans and inspect contents to determine what foods cooks are wasting, what guests are not eating, and if flatware is being thrown away with trash.

- **FIFO System:** Label and date all prepared items to ensure food is used on a first-in, first-out (FIFO) basis, minimizing spoilage and poor flavors. Regularly inspect food dates to ensure proper rotation.

- **Establish Recipe Yields:** Determine recipe yields for all purchased foods.

- **Avoid Over-Preparation:** Avoid over-preparing fragile food that quickly dries out or spoils easily.

- **Minor Repairs:** Make minor repairs as needed to equipment and facilities to avoid the high cost and delay of professional repairs and costly breakdowns.

TENTH KEY TO $UCCESS
SHADOW COACH YOUR STAFF'S PERFORMANCE

Ensure Your Effective Procedures and Methods Are Used.

Not managing staff members is the easy way to run a restaurant. Unless you make a conscious effort to know how your staff is performing their duties, it is easy to assume they are following your procedures or have the necessary common sense. You can't hire people who know how to run a restaurant as staff members. If you are comfortable with them doing things their way, you will be providing your guests with an inconsistent, amateurish experience, and you are doomed to failure. Letting staff members decide the way they clean, greet, serve, and prepare food for guests is the #1 reason restaurants fail.

Shadow coaching is a method to ensure that the procedures and methods for running a restaurant that you have adopted are being properly used. These procedures and methods are the foundation of your business's operation and the linchpin of your restaurant's success. Without control of these elements, a restaurant is at risk of failure due to a lack of guest satisfaction and low patronage. Correct execution is essential for survival in today's competitive environment. Your success cannot be left to chance or the good fortune of hiring talented people. If systems are not monitored, they can easily be modified or abbreviated by your staff, losing their effectiveness.

ROLE OF THE SHADOW COACH

- **Thorough Understanding:** The Shadow Coach must thoroughly understand every step of every system they are accountable for, to provide continuous orientation and influence to staff members. Staff often need help executing their jobs correctly, and coaches must learn each position for which they are accountable.

- **Support and Training:** If supervisors do not understand system steps, they cannot support staff with the details. Staff will sense their ignorance and improve their job performance. Shadow coaches should perform job systems long enough to know what subordinates are asked to do.

- **Regular Review:** The Shadow Coach should review the restaurant's handbook, general operations, and staff and manager operations manuals often to ensure an understanding of system details. They should use the Tell 'em, Show 'em, Check 'em training system to train staff members.

- **Vigorous Implementation:** Shadow Coaches must implement system changes with vigor. They should make notes to remember systems and use systems to answer all questions, referring to operations manuals to reinforce them as the source of all methods. Document all work in detail for consistency throughout the operation. Verbal processes are easily misunderstood, soon forgotten, or changed, leading to inconsistencies in products and services.

TEAMWORK AND SUCCESS

The goal of a restaurant is to provide high-quality meals and excellent service to guests while staying within food and labor costs to make a profit. This goal can only be achieved with the cooperation and support of all staff members. Just as a football franchise succeeds when players and staff form a cohesive team, a restaurant succeeds when its staff forms a solid working team.

Modern training methods must be used that are formalized and standardized to succeed with adding enjoyable ingredients to your recipes and systems.

SHADOW COACHING: ENSURING PROPER USE OF PROCEDURES AND METHODS

Management's Role in Shadow Coaching: Management must shadow coach the work by observing details and providing clear instructions to develop a high-performance staff. Continuous feedback about the flow of work is essential until each staff member thoroughly understands their job.

Why is Shadow Coaching Essential?

- **High Staff Turnover:** Due to high staff turnover, an inexperienced labor market, and a short-term mentality, shadow coaching ensures consistent performance.

- **Avoiding Complacency:** Staff members may minimize their duties and eliminate awkward or tedious steps. Shadow coaching ensures adherence to proper procedures and methods.

- **Guest Feedback:** Guests will not train or coach your staff for you. They often remain silent and hide their true feelings, leading staff to believe they are satisfied even when they may be disappointed or unimpressed.

Benefits of Shadow Coaching

- Ensures every operating system is used correctly by management and staff.

- Develops friendly, orchestrated service techniques to exceed guest expectations.

- Guarantees work is done correctly, bringing guests back often and reducing costs.

Characteristics of an Effective Shadow Coach

- **Enthusiastic and Passionate:** Committed to bringing guests back by helping staff members improve and feel the excitement of being their best.

- **Positive Feedback:** Provides positive feedback for correct work and delegates tasks without assuming results.

- **Follow-Up:** Follows up on issues and influences staff to perform correctly.

- **Avoids Doing Staff's Work:** An inexperienced manager may try to do their staff's work, preventing them from influencing correct systems and understanding staff actions. This can lead to discretionary decisions and varied actions by staff, resulting in questionable outcomes.

Shadow Coaching as a Partnership

- **Training:** Particularly important for inexperienced staff. Management works with staff to achieve system results, acting as the coach and expert on how the work is performed.

- **Influence:** Coaches teach staff how to improve work quality and quantity until they perform their jobs correctly. Success is measured by the coach's influence and team-building ability.

- **Welcomed Coaching:** Staff members, especially new hires, welcome shadow coaching that influences and challenges them without pestering them. Poorly trained, experienced staff may initially resist changes, but effective coaching provides high productivity and job success.

Key Responsibilities of a Shadow Coach

- Puts themselves in a position to observe staff in action.

- *Give praise and thanks to the staff for correct behavior to encourage continuation.*

- Corrects and encourages staff to perform work correctly.

- Addresses poor productivity to meet labor cost standards.

- Follows up on corrective feedback to reinforce correct work or provide additional support.

- Continually thanks and encourages staff for correct work.

- Is an expert at the work and makes experts out of staff members.

- Maintains influence over staff even when not present.

- Has good communication skills and teaches effectively.

A well-coached staff member knows their work and feels supported by their coach, who treats them respectfully, fairly, and courteously. The coach summarizes work in shift reports for partner managers, ensuring that guests receive quality products and services, which is key to their return.

LEARNING TO BE AN EFFECTIVE SHADOW COACH

As new managers learn to be effective shadow coaches, they may need to adopt new strategies. One good definition of insanity is to keep doing the same things repeatedly and expect different results. The challenge is not how to get new and innovative ideas into your mind but how to get the old ones out. To achieve better results, managers must change their perspective on the work of being a manager.

Shadow Coaching Systems: Shadow coaching systems are performed while working the manager's path. Every staff member should be shadow-coached to ensure they know your professional systems so the work is done correctly and quickly. The manager will know the specific work habits of every subordinate and the methods they are using. New staff members should be able to carry a full workload within a few days (i.e., 50% first full shift, 60% second shift, 70% third shift, 80% fourth shift, 90% fifth shift, and 100% thereafter). Socializing slows the flow of work and decreases productivity. Having an excessive number of staff members on duty or allowing them too much time to do their jobs encourages socializing, which distracts from guest service and productivity.

Exhibiting Passion for Guest Service: Shadow coaches exhibit a passion for individual guest service by using systems to bring guests back. Your staff members will imitate you. Note staff members' punctuality, compliment timeliness, and discourage tardiness. Repeated tardiness should be addressed. Inspect uniforms and personal appearance. Assign staff members to their workstations. Be friendly, but do not over-socialize or seek staff members' approval on or off duty.

Maintaining Authority: It is impossible to be a pal and manage someone effectively. It will weaken your authority and make it difficult to give corrective feedback. Staff members who socialize with a manager often seek favors and special treatment. An effective manager seeks respect rather than popularity.

Governing Coaching Communications: Let systems govern coaching communications. Be a source of ongoing orientation. Staff members have a lot to learn and can easily forget details. Your authority will grow as staff members develop confidence in you. Thanking subordinates for doing a system correctly is an excellent way to provide positive feedback and strengthen your position of authority.

Ensuring Compliance: Don't soften compliance by making light of systems or by creating a casual atmosphere. Don't overuse orders and commands or give too much feedback at once, as it might be perceived as pestering. "Do it because I say so" results in a tense climate.

Respect and Confidentiality: Don't use your superior's name to "get results." It weakens your position and diminishes the respect staff members have for you as a manager. Comments from your manager about staff members are meant to help you be more effective, not less, and should be kept confidential.

Fair Treatment: Treat all your staff members equally without favoritism. Don't give special treatment or have pets. Be dependable and keep your promises about workstation assignments, schedules, time off requests, pay rate changes, etc. Provide continuous feedback so your staff members are accustomed to your communications. This causes them to seek your approval and acceptance. Honest feedback is usually 90% positive.

Attention to New Staff: Give special attention and extra time to new staff members. It helps them effectively perform systems and quickly integrates them into your team. Be consistent every day. Don't bring a bad mood or personal problems to work. Unpredictability makes staff members feel insecure.

Resolving Disagreements: Resolve disagreements or bad feelings with your staff members—report continuing disagreements to your supervisor for resolution. Never complain about another manager, staff member, or situation to your staff members. This creates negative attitudes and is counterproductive. Be calm and patient. Be an emotional rock in the face of chaos and confusion. Don't become panic-stricken in the face of pressure.

Coach with an iron fist and a velvet glove."

–Disney Institute

"If the student hasn't learned, the teacher hasn't taught."

–Siegfried Engelmann, educationalist

Importance of Monitoring Work Details: Your staff members may misunderstand your professional systems and resort to amateur shortcuts. Therefore, management must closely monitor staff members' work to ensure they follow the correct systems and produce the desired results.

KEY PRACTICES FOR EFFECTIVE MONITORING

- **Comfortable Presence:** Develop a comfortable manner of being in the workspace without physically doing their work or mentally drifting. Be complimentary and friendly while remaining observant of the details and manner in which staff members perform their work.

- **Focused Observation:** Follow your path, stop, and concentrate on one staff member at a time. Avoid jumping around or being easily distracted, as this can cause you to lose awareness and become reactive rather than proactive.

- **Behavior Recognition:** Recognize correct and incorrect staff member behavior. Watch the "work zone" where hands take orders, clean, prepare, and serve food. Never walk past a staff member without noticing what they are doing.

Performance Assessment

- **System Adherence:** Determine if they are performing their work according to your professional systems.

- **Pace and Conditions:** Assess if they are working at their best pace and maintaining general conditions (clean, sanitary, organized, clutter-free, well-stocked workstations; appropriate appearance and attitude; proper hand washing and food handling; waste and stock levels; lighting and temperature; equipment use and condition; meals, breaks, honesty; water and electricity use; other systems).

Supervision Without Interference

- **Super Vision:** Stay out of production to have "Super Vision," observing work freely without being encumbered. If you must engage in physical production, keep one eye on staff members' hands and one eye on yours. Avoid getting in their way while watching their work.

Shadow Coaching Standards

- **New Staff Members:** Every new staff member will be shadow-coached as needed to ensure they know and are performing their duties correctly.

- **Experienced Staff:** Staff members will not be left to their own methods unless their manager can guarantee correct performance based on previous training and shadow coaching.

  People like to work for the best and be part of a winning team.

  "Mary, I appreciate your friendliness. It attracts Guests and makes you very important to the organization." (Pause) "I'm glad you're working here."

  "Sally, this salad is perfect and looks great." "I know our Guests will be impressed with it."

  "Warren, you have really improved on your grill speed and organization. You are becoming one of our best cooks." (Pause) "Thanks for working so hard."

PRAISE CORRECT STAFF MEMBER BEHAVIOR

The Power of Praise: Praise causes staff members to respect you as a manager and encourages them. Staff members usually do the majority of their work correctly and, therefore, should receive more positive than negative feedback. Praise correct behavior in a way that encourages staff members to continue following systems correctly, making them feel appreciated and successful in their work.

Key Practices for Praising Staff

- **Specific Praise:** Thank staff members for doing a system correctly by giving specific praise. Tell them exactly what they did right. Reward the most minor improvements.

- **Nonverbal Praise:** Use nonverbal praise such as a smile, nod, wink, or thumbs up for emphasis.

- **Hustle Buck Rewards:** Issue a hustle buck reward to staff members who continuously hustle and provide fast service. Staff members appreciate it when you recognize their hustle and will work to become even faster.

- **Immediate Feedback:** Give praise for good behavior honestly, sincerely, and immediately.

Examples

Recognize Outstanding Performance:

Shower staff members who perform your systems well with recognition and attention. Make quality guest service and reliability an obsession with your staff members. Recount stories about how staff member heroes served guests well, developing a sense of belonging and appreciation.

Welcome and Thank Staff Members:

Welcome staff members to every shift and thank them when they leave. Remember, they are working as volunteers for you. Say "Hi" when they come on shift and make them feel welcome. Recognize them with a smile and friendliness as you move around the restaurant. Show them that you like them as a person. Be courteous and good-natured as you work with them. Say "Thank You" often, especially when they leave their shift.

Sample Staff Member Recognitions:

- **Staff Member of the Shift:** Recognize one outstanding staff member every shift based on performance. This is a great way to acknowledge a staff member's outstanding attitude. Tell them you have selected them as the "staff member of the shift" and thank them for their good work. Document the recognition on your Shift Report.

- **Staff Member of the Month:** Select a "Staff Member of the Month" from the "Staff Members of the Shift" for the past month. Take into account feedback reports and consider those with outstanding attitudes. Prepare a certificate of appreciation and present the award in the presence of other staff members.

RECOGNIZE OUTSTANDING STAFF MEMBERS AS "STARS" OR "HEROES" IDEAS

Recognize staff members who meet Star standards by performing their work according to systems 100% of the time. They are dependable, show up on time, work full shifts, and always look professional in freshly laundered, pressed uniforms. They exemplify great attitudes, are outgoing and friendly with guests and staff members, and hustle to provide extra-mile service to bring guests back. Add a star to their name tag, give them a star pin, and provide an hourly bonus. Post their picture on the "Star" or "Hero's" bulletin board.

Minimizing Incorrect Behavior

Unprofessional (amateur) behavior should be minimized in a manner that encourages staff members to perform their work correctly. Correct minor errors by bringing them to the staff member's attention and reminding them of the correct method. Be specific and clear about what they did wrong.

Examples of Minor Corrections

- "Bill, make sure you always wipe the edge of the dinner plate. It makes a better-looking meal presentation."

- "Mary, remember always to smile. It makes guests feel welcome."

Explain to staff members how the system they fail to follow brings guests back or controls costs. This helps them understand the importance of the system. Train staff members to maintain standards on their own. For example, instead of telling someone to clean up the floor around their workstation, instruct them to always to keep the floor area clean.

Additional Steps

- Reprimand continued incorrect behavior in private.
- Provide additional training and review the operations manual if needed.
- Create consequences that encourage the use of correct systems, such as praise, reprimand, or retraining.
- Demonstrate correct procedures and explain why incorrect ones are unacceptable.
- Get a commitment from the staff member to change their behavior.
- Reaffirm that you think well of them but not their behavior.
- Understand that once a reprimand is over, it's over.

Follow-Up on Corrective Feedback

When you ask a subordinate to correct specific work, expect them to follow through. It's essential to follow up and recognize them when they change their behavior.

Key Practices for Follow-Up

- **Observation:** Closely observe the staff member's performance to determine if they correct their work.

- **Praise:** Praise them when they perform the work correctly.

- **Progressive Discipline:** Provide progressive discipline if they continue to perform poorly.

- **Commitment:** Reaffirm their commitment to performing the system correctly.

- **Understanding:** Determine why they do not follow instructions and express confidence in their ability to do their job correctly.

- **Review:** Review procedures, methods, and work standards.

- **Consequences:** Warn them about the consequences of poor work.

- **Increasing Consequences:** Raise the stakes for continued poor performance by increasing negative consequences.

- **Closer Supervision:** Provide closer supervision to assist them in breaking a bad habit by increasing encouragement and positive reinforcement.

WRITTEN WARNING FOR UNRESOLVED ISSUES

When follow-up attempts fail, and the staff member does not achieve productivity standards or quality results, issuing a written warning is necessary. Here are the steps to take:

Key Steps for Issuing a Written Warning

- **Document Specific Issues:** Clearly state the specific productivity standards or quality results that are not being met. Provide examples and reference previous feedback.

- **Explain Consequences:** Outline the consequences of not meeting standards, including potential disciplinary actions if improvements are not made.

- **Provide Support:** Offer additional training or resources to help the staff member improve. Show a willingness to support their development.

- **Set Clear Expectations:** Clearly define the expectations moving forward. Specify measurable goals and a timeline for achieving them.

- **Follow-Up Plan:** Establish a follow-up plan to review progress. Schedule regular check-ins to monitor improvement and provide ongoing feedback.

- **Acknowledge Positive Aspects:** Recognize any positive aspects of the staff member's performance to maintain a balanced approach.

Example Warning

Date:

To: [Staff Member's Name]

Subject: Written Warning for Performance Improvement

Dear [Staff Member's Name],

This written warning is to address the ongoing issues with your performance formally. Despite previous discussions and feedback, you have not achieved the productivity standards or quality results expected in your role. Expressly, the following issues have been noted:

- [Detail specific issues with examples]

- [Reference previous feedback and attempts to resolve]

It is essential to meet the following expectations to improve your performance:

- [Clearly define expectations and measurable goals]

- [Specify the timeline for achieving these goals]

Failure to meet these expectations may result in further disciplinary actions, up to and including termination of employment. We are committed to supporting your success and offer additional training and resources to help you improve. Please schedule a meeting with your manager to discuss this matter further and outline an improvement plan.

Sincerely, [Manager's Name]

"Wealth does not bring about excellence, but excellence brings about wealth and all other public and private blessings . . . . ."

–Socrates

ADJUST YOUR STAFF MEMBERS' MINDSETS

Addressing Common Mindsets: Inexperienced restaurant staff members might believe that once a guest is in the restaurant, they are committed and will return with regularity. This mindset can lead to staff unknowingly taking advantage of guests by not avoiding inconsistencies in service. Staff may prioritize their own challenges and personal needs over guests', leading to neglect.

Key Challenges for Staff

- **Getting Guests to Return:** Present the challenge of getting guests to return with increased frequency every day the restaurant is open.

- **Measuring Success:** Use systems to attract guests and ensure they are executed precisely. Compare customer counts against the same period the previous year, under similar conditions, to measure success.

Understanding Sales and Performance

- **Sales Reflection:** Today's sales result from yesterday's performance. Tomorrow's sales result from today's performance. The restaurant works today to impact tomorrow's sales.

- **Training Importance:** Most restaurant problems and closures stem from hiring untrained staff. Train staff to know food production and service steps and standards, ensuring every product and service is perfect.

- **Quality Control:** Quality control processes ensure that every aspect of your dining experience meets high standards consistently. This process includes monitoring food preparation to guarantee freshness, flavor, and safety, as well as maintaining cleanliness in the kitchen and dining areas. It also involves evaluating staff performance, ensuring excellent service, and addressing customer feedback promptly to uphold the restaurant's reputation. Quality control is vital for delivering a reliable and satisfying experience.

- **Spot Checks:** Spot-check products during production and before delivery to guests to ensure quality standards.

- **Prevent Defects:** Never let guests be the only inspectors of defective products or sub-standard service. Teach staff the product and service quality standards and how to meet them.

- **Utilize Reports:** Use quality control reports timely. Inspect purchased materials upon arrival to ensure they meet specifications.

- **Standard Delivery:** Deliver menu items exactly according to recipes and standards—rework nonstandard products during production to minimize labor waste and service delays.

- **Stop Below-Standard Products:** Train staff to stop serving below-standard products, including those with nonstandard ingredients, wrong size or shape, wrong texture or temperature, wrong taste, and frozen or freezer-burned.

Building Loyalty

Experience Over Price: Customers base their loyalty on the experience (Value) they receive, not just price or product. Failure to meet their increasing demands will result in losing customers.

"There is only one boss. The customer. And he can fire everybody in the company from the chairman on down, simply by spending his money somewhere else.

–Sam Walton, Founder of Walmart

TRAIN YOUR STAFF THAT RESTAURANT GUESTS ARE YOUR BOSS, THEREFORE THEIR BOSS

Understanding the Guest-Centric Approach: Managers may want to be in business to be their own boss, which sounds great. However, the reality is that they indirectly answer to every one of your customers. They may now have 10,000 bosses who won't directly tell them what to do. They will have to figure it out before they fire them one by one by leaving as customers.

"It's not who you know. It's what you know that counts." You mustn't be a political organization catering to whims. All power flows directly from guests. They provide job security for those who create enjoyment for them. All decisions, including hiring and promotions, must be based on what's good for the guest.

Prioritizing Guest Experience Over Profits: Your boss must not be making profits and cuttingting costs. Decisions should reflect the long-term benefits for your guests. It's shortsighted to think of current profits at the expense of the guest's experience, including cleanliness, decor, food taste and appearance, service style, and friendliness. Everything should prioritize guests over profits: *"If you take care of guests, they will take care of you."*

Cost Considerations: Providing better service, food, decor, and cleanliness usually costs more. Cutting costs is easy if you don't focus on the guest's experience. It's important to make a profit, but cutting costs must not compromise the guest experience. There are successful operations that offer a cheaper price, like Little Caesars Pizza, providing an inexpensive product at a lower price. There's a market for a "no frills" experience appealing to some people.

GIVING DIRECTIVES EFFECTIVELY

Characteristics of an Effective Shadow Coach

- **Confident and Direct:** Takes immediate action when confronted with a problem.

- **Sincere Liking for People:** Likes people but does not let subordinates control decisions.

- **Effective Communication:** Provides information in a manner that staff readily understands, accepts, and executes.

- **Consistent Communication Style:** Avoids treating staff members coldly, using ridicule, or speaking indirectly.

- **Problem-Focused:** Attacks the problem, not the person.

- **Clear Instructions:** Don't assume others will figure out what they want. Uses "I" to give directives and "We" to indicate teamwork.

- **Frequent Thank-Yous:** Says thank you often and makes eye contact when possible.

- **Comprehensive Directives:** Devotes time to really show, tell, encourage, answer questions, and follow-up.

Using Different Types of Directives

- **Requests:** Direct staff members in everyday situations. Easy to learn and use.

- Examples: "Tom, when you get a chance, would you clean that sink better?" "Jan, will you come in early tomorrow."

- **Commands:** Used in emergencies, for strict control, immediate action, or when tasks are simple.

- Examples: "Mary, sort this silverware and take it immediately to the line." "Jim, go help on the grill." "Bill, answer the phone, please."

- **Calls for Volunteers:** Assign beyond-the-call-of-duty tasks or release staff from shifts occasionally. Avoid overuse.

- **Assertive and Respectful Communication:** Speak assertively and respectfully, thanking staff often for professional work.

By adopting these practices, you can create a positive and effective work environment, ensuring staff members understand that the guest experience is paramount and providing clear, effective directives. Extinction theory: *good work that goes unacknowledged will gradually disappear*

ACTIVE MANAGEMENT PREVENTS "IN-THE-WEEDS" SITUATIONS

When a restaurant provides poor-tasting food, slow or unfriendly service, or unclean conditions, it is "in the weeds." These situations arise when the speed of service is stalled, facilities are allowed to become dirty, and food preparation is sloppy or unavailable. "In the weeds" situations are emergencies that require immediate action to eliminate further mistakes or delays.

Examples of Being "In the Weeds"

- Guests are not greeted properly or served in a friendly manner.

- There is an open table, and the guest is not seated immediately.

- A server does not greet a guest at the table within 60 seconds.

- Take-out guest service is stalled for any reason.

- Dine-in order is not taken in less than 2 minutes, or the guest is ready with folded menus.

- Dine-in order is not entered into the computer within 60 seconds of being taken.

- Order preparation is not started immediately or completed in less than 11 minutes.

- Beverages are not served in less than 2 minutes after taking the order.

- Salad/soup/dessert is not served in less than 5 minutes after taking the order.

- A guest is waiting for their check or change for over 2 minutes.

- A call-in guest is put on hold, or the phone rings three times or more.

- A menu item is not available.

Proactive Management Strategies

- **Ensure Proper Greetings:** Train staff to greet guests promptly and warmly.

- **Efficient Seating:** Implement a system to seat guests immediately when tables are available.

- **Prompt Server Response:** Ensure servers greet and welcome guests at their tables within 60 seconds.

- **Streamline Take-Out Service:** Monitor take-out service to prevent delays.

- **Fast Order Taking:** Ensure dine-in orders are taken within 2 minutes and guests with folded menus are prioritized.

- **Timely Order Entry:** Make sure orders are entered into the computer promptly.

- **Efficient Order Preparation:** Start order preparation immediately and aim to complete it in less than 11 minutes.

- **Quick Beverage Service:** Serve beverages within minutes of taking the order.

- **Timely Salad/Soup/Dessert Service:** Serve salads, soups, or desserts within 5 minutes of taking the order.

- **Speedy Check/Change Delivery:** Ensure guests receive their check or change within 2 minutes.

- **Responsive Phone Service:** Answer calls promptly, ideally before the third ring.

- **Menu Availability:** Regularly check inventory to ensure menu items are available.

TIME YOUR KITCHEN ORDER PREPARATION

By implementing these proactive management strategies, you can prevent "in the weeds" situations, ensuring a smooth and pleasant dining experience for your guests.

Absolutely! It's crucial to recognize that most guests won't voice their complaints, making it all the more important for management to be proactive in identifying and addressing issues. When guests are waiting for service beyond a reasonable time, your restaurant is considered to be "In the Weeds." Here are some managerial solutions to prevent and manage these situations effectively:

Managerial Solutions to Avoid "In-The-Weeds" Situations

- **Stay on a Supervisory Path:** Continuously monitor staff to recognize when they need assistance.

- **Immediate Action:** Act promptly to correct or minimize problems and assist staff with guest service. Resolve issues as soon as possible, such as rushing orders, taking orders, expediting seating, or helping with food production.

- **Support Staff Members:** Never leave an "In-the-Weeds" situation without addressing it. Coordinate trained staff positions or personally help when staff members are stretched beyond their capacity.

- **In and Out of Production:** Get involved in production to resolve issues but quickly return to supervising to maintain overall control.

- **Acknowledge Mistakes or Delays:** Apologize to guests before they complain using a script like: "I apologize for the [issue]. I will correct the problem. I appreciate your patience and understanding." This reassures guests that you are aware of the problem and committed to resolving it, enhancing their confidence in your service standards.

- **Treat All Guest Problems Seriously:** Address guest issues from their perspective and provide immediate, thorough responses to complaints.

Standards to Adopt

- **Control of Work:** Ensure every staff member is always in control of their work.

- **Manager Assistance:** Managers should assist staff members "in the weeds" as soon as possible.

- **Document Events:** Record "in-the-weeds" events in a shift report for future reference.

- **Apologies and Corrections:** Guests who receive below-standard service or experience an unfavorable situation should receive an apology and corrective action from a manager. Consider offering a complimentary dessert or other compensation if their order takes longer than a specified time to prepare and serve.

"I went to a fancy French restaurant called Deja Vu. The head waiter said, 'Don't I know you?'

–Rod Schmidt

YOUR PERSONAL GROWTH AND BUSINESS STRATEGIES

Striving for Success in the Restaurant Business

Success in the restaurant business combines striving for personal growth and excelling as an entrepreneur. Continually aiming for personal excellence will aid you in your quest for success as a restaurateur. Operating a restaurant can serve as the perfect laboratory for overcoming personal challenges and growing as an individual.

"The only way we can move from where we are now to where we would like to be is to accept where we are now."

–Stephen R Covey, author and motivational speaker

Characteristics of Successful Entrepreneur –Bill Dyer, Brigham Young University

1. The ability to take risks.

2. The desire to compete.

3. The ability to handle stress.

4. The ability to make work fun.

5. The ability to solve problems creatively.

6. The ability to recognize opportunities.

7. A high level of commitment to the business.

8. Goal oriented.

9. A sense of realistic optimism.

Working with Partners –Bill Dyer, Brigham Young University

1. Choose a partner with complementary goals and skills.

2. Clarify roles and responsibilities.

3. Create a buy-sell agreement.

4. Determine where the money is coming from.

5. Set up lines of communication.

6. Develop mechanisms to handle conflict.

7. Decide how to decide.

8. Determine fairness of time and commitment.

9. Put it in writing.

10. Get appropriate help when needed.

Enjoying Workflow –by Migaly Csikszentmihalyi

"What exactly is flow? Imagine for a moment that you are running a race. Your attention is focused on the movements of your body, the power of your muscles, the force of your lungs, and the feel of the street beneath your feet. You are living in the moment, utterly absorbed in the present activity. Time seems to fall away. You are tired, but you barely notice.

There are people who find their work exhilarating and who perform it at their best. The key to that exhilaration is not the task itself but the special state of mind they create as they experience work in a state of "flow." The enjoyment of flow causes them to do their best work at whatever they are doing.

Flow is a state of mind we are in when we are fully engaged and totally absorbed in our work. Flow is enhanced when we are being stretched in new and challenging ways. This challenge so engages us that we lose ourselves in our work. We become totally concentrating and feel "out of touch with time". In this flow state of mind, we can handle everything effortlessly, easily adapting to changing demands and circumstances.

The enjoyment of "flow" is the ultimate motivator. Activities we love draw us in because we get into flow as we pursue them. Of course, what gives each person such pleasure varies depending on his or her work. When we work in flow, the motivation is built in and our work is a delight; a manager might become totally absorbed in creating great service for Guests, seeing them Enjoy fresh made food, supervising cooks while they prepare delicious sandwiches that surely Guests will Enjoy or training a host to cause Guest to feel welcome.

The enjoyment of flow is a newly discovered realization about what motivates people at work. Incentive such a work reviews, promotions, bonuses as well as a basic salary are important ways to "keep score". But the most powerful motivators are internal not external. We feel better doing work we love rather than work we do only because we are rewarded for it. When doing a task for the pleasure of it, our moods are upbeat and happy.

When doing something merely for the pay, we can be bored, disinterested, even annoyed. We are more unhappy if our tasks are stressful or burdensome. It feels better doing what we have a passion for, even if there are less rewards.

Emotions are what move us to pursue our goals; they rule our motivation, and our motives in turn determine our perceptions and shape our actions. Great work starts with a great feeling towards our work.

When people are in flow, they often make difficult work look easy. While enjoying the flow they can be engaged in exceptionally demanding tasks, and yet their brain is operating with a minimal level of activity or expenditure of energy. The reason is when we are bored or anxious, our brain activity is diffused; the brain itself is operating at a high level of activity, although poorly focused, with our brain cells firing in irrelevant and disconnected ways. During flow the brain is efficient in its pattern of firing.

Motivated people may Enjoy "flow" 50 percent of the time while working. The most common emotional state reported during leisure time is apathy. For top performers, flow occurs in work that is most critical to their goals rather than in fascinating diversions. For top performers excellence and pleasure in work are one and the same."

How to Manage by Walking Around –by Janis Allen

"MBWA, or managing by walking around, has become a popular idea for managers. A little bit of knowledge, however, is very dangerous here. The idea is to walk around and talk to people. But the question is. Talk about what? When you do walk around, the most obvious things that jump out at you are the problems you see. After all, managers got where they are by solving problems and noticing what needs to be corrected. When it comes to people, though, if you spend most of your time talking to them about what's wrong and needs to be corrected, you will soon be seen as someone to hide from, not someone the staff members look forward to seeing. Here are some guidelines for making "walking around" positive and productive.

Look for simple behavioral patterns you can reinforce, such as someone's going out of their way to greet a customer and smiling or someone's offering help to a co-worker. Scan the room for sights that make you feel proud and then tell the person who is responsible. That will lead your associates to look forward to seeing you and will make your own day as well as theirs."

PRIORITIZING TASKS TO ENSURE EFFICIENT GUEST SERVICE

Performing first-priority work expeditiously eliminates delays in guest service and is essential for retaining guests. It's vital to shift resources from second-priority work to assist with first-priority work as needed.

First Priority Work

- Greeting, seating, and taking guests' orders in person or on the phone.

- Preparing orders and keeping self-service bars fully stocked.

- Serving orders.

- Collecting and accounting for payments.

- Clearing tables and keeping the dining room spotless.

- Storing received refrigerated and frozen food.

- Preparing out-of-stock food, supplies, and dishware.

Second Priority Work

- Receiving and stocking materials.

- Preparing backup food stock.

- Washing dishes.

- Cleaning equipment, walls, fixtures, and closing sections.

- Keeping records and making reports.

- Hiring, interviewing, training, scheduling, and performing reviews.

- Meeting, planning, taking breaks, and having meals.

Staff members performing second-priority work should be shifted to first-priority tasks when potential delays occur. Staff members should be trained to perform at least one first-priority job to help eliminate delays in guest service.

"Simply put, where management is about getting people to do something for you, Leadership is about getting people to do something for themselves."

–Monty F. Moran, Chipotle CEO

Ten Steps to Operational Success –Aaron Donatello URA –Hot Plate Publication

"Each individual operation has its own critical success factor-those products, people or services that produce the greatest contribution to profit. Skilled operators are aware of their own critical success factors and dutifully assign high priority to these items daily. Here are 10 important steps to restaurant success you may want to consider in your operation.

1: Know your daily plan before you enter the restaurant.

Good planners never start a day unprepared. Some prepare lists for the next day before they leave their unit at night. They can then go home and relax, confident that when they return the next morning, they will be ahead of the game with their daily plan waiting. Other operators use recorders to tape their plan while driving to work. They too, save precious time with a well-organized agenda. So, stay ahead, plan tomorrow's list today.

2: See that the job gets done.

Following up on a project is more important than initiating it. It is better to be known as a hard-nose persistent operator and make sure that the job gets done than to be caught off-guard and forged to make excuses later.

3: Remember that you bank dollars not percentages.

Most operators are looking to lower their food cost percentages, but this should not be done without looking at profit contributions. The mathematical difference between a menu items' product cost and its selling price is its profit contribution. Management will do well to encourage the sale of high-profit contribution items regardless of food cost percentages.

4: Serve your hot food on hot plates, cold food on cold plates.

Even the best-prepared meals can be spoiled if not served at the proper temperature. The closer the temperature of the service ware to the food, the better is the chances of the food maintaining that temperature.

5: Remember people eat with their eyes.

If it doesn't look good, don't serve it. People should say or think, "Wow, this is great," when they receive their order.

6: Buy the best products available.

Don't accept any products that doesn't meet your specifications and standards. You can't make a silk purse out of a sow's ear, as the maxim goes. If an operation starts with quality products, there is a good chance that it can finish with quality product.

7: Give feedback on the spot.

When you see staff members doing a particularly good job, tell them on the spot. The closer the feedback is to the behavior, the greater its impact.

8: Acknowledge your Guests with a smile at the door, the bar and the table.

The first thing people see or experience exerts a strong influence on their final impression of a restaurant. From the time the Guests enter the establishment until their presence is acknowledged, seconds seem like minutes (jeopardizing your chances to make a good impression). A simple greeting from anyone, such as, "Hello, how are you?" will lessen the burden of waiting.

9: Develop your name recall skills.

This is a key to building repeat business. Guests have egos and like recognition, particularly if they are with friends. People with Guests will go out of their way to go to a place where they are known.

10: You can't afford to have anyone leave your restaurant unhappy.

It has often been said that when someone has a good experience at a restaurant, they tell three people; but when the experience is bad, they tell seven. That is why total dedication to customer satisfaction on the part of every staff member is vital to the success of your restaurant. What impression should your Guests leave with? One, which compels them to tell all their friends what a great place, you have!"

STRIVING TO CHANGE FOR THE BETTER

Striving: To make efforts, to labor hard.

Change: To alter, modify; make slight alterations; to substitute one thing in place of another; to give up for something else; to make different; to convert; to vary; to pass from one phase to another; to shift; diversification, growth.

Better: To improve; to better our situation; to increase the number of good qualities; to improve the condition of worldly welfare; to surpass excellently; to a higher or greater degree.

Like all businesses, you must find better ways and means of doing things or face going out of business. There is no magic formula for success. There is no guarantee you will continue to enjoy your present favorable circumstances without future change and improvement. You can very quickly become obsolete in a world changing at dizzying rates.

Objectives

- Improved staff member job satisfaction.

- Improved guest satisfaction.

- Improved restaurant profitability and return on investment

Methods of Improvement

- **Provide Positive Feedback:** Offer more feedback to staff members on performance and results.

- **Share Responsibility:** Share responsibility with staff members capable of participating due to job maturity and competency.

- **Compensate Fairly:** Base compensation on long-term and short-term performance results.

- **Improve Facilities and Equipment:** Invest in facilities and equipment that yield an acceptable return on investment.

- **Enhance Personnel Management:** Employ better personnel management methods, procedures, and philosophies.

- **Improve Communication:** Strengthen communication efforts between management and staff members.

Negative attitudes can easily spoil the working environment and the job satisfaction of many staff members. Each staff member is responsible for discussing their concerns with their fellow staff members constructively. They should talk to their immediate manager to resolve concerns quickly before jeopardizing their job security and the working environment.

Appreciate and recognize when staff members contribute to improving your restaurant through their daily efforts. Working together as a team, through improved communication and understanding, can and will bring continued success.

"Speech is power: speech is to persuade, to convert to compel."

–Ralph Waldo Emerson, philosopher

THOUGHTS ON GOAL SETTING

Goals must be realistic or possible and must be a stretch. Goal setting involves making commitments and deals with people. Internalize your goals and commit to them. Get in the habit of establishing and achieving goals.

- **Be Prepared:** Plan and set specific goals. Implement – determine what to do. Execute – follow-up. Review – analyze the results.

- **Planned Events:** A goal is a planned-for event. Goals without plans do not work, while goals with plans create tranquility. Failure to achieve results breaks resolve.

- **Begin with the End in Mind:** When a goal is valued, it becomes a priority. When goals are valued together, prioritizing takes place. Prioritizing is the process of determining the precedence of events.

- **Specificity Leads to Success:** When we deal in generalities, we rarely succeed. When we deal in specifics, we rarely fail.

- **Clearly Defined Goals:** In the absence of clearly defined goals, we are forced to concentrate on an activity and become enslaved to it.

- **Realistic Steps:** If your next goal is realistic, your whole goal is realistic. If your next goal is not clearly defined, you have no goals.

- **Evolution, Not Revolution:** Our goals in life should be about evolution, not revolution.

- **Daily Plan:** Program yourself to have a good day plan.

- **Progress and Clarity:** If you are not making the progress you would like to and are capable of, it is simply because your goals are not clearly defined.

- **Mutual Work:** When you set goals for yourself, they work in two ways: you work on them, and they work on you.

- **Self-motivation:** Goal setting is the strongest human force for self-motivation.

- **High Goals:** The human scene is crowded with people who have gone as far as they are going simply because their goals are not high enough.

- **Prelude to Action:** The goals people set for themselves are a prelude to action, a track to run on, and a course to take. They express the noblest quality of humanity. No one ever accomplishes anything of consequence without a goal.

- **Belief in Success:** Once you have set a goal, believe firmly and unequivocally that you will reach it. The stronger your belief, the more rapid your progress will be.

- **Shaping Destiny:** Each of us is born to shape a destiny for ourselves. The depth and extent of that destiny are measured by the personal goals we set.

- **No Regrets:** Do not waste time with regret for the goals you failed to set in the past. Goal direction begins today for the successful future you can create.

Being engaged with guests is crucial for growing sales. Disengagement leads to declining sales.

- **Understanding Guest Expectations:** Working in the restaurant business means understanding that guests will not return often unless they are rewarded with pleasant experiences. This includes fast, attentive, and friendly service, delicious food that looks delightful, clean and sanitary environments, comfortable conditions, and well-maintained facilities.

- **Avoiding Assumptions:** Working around the restaurant business means assuming that guests <u>will</u> return even after enduring unpleasant experiences. These can include slow, indifferent service, marginal food quality, unsanitary and uncomfortable environments, unsightly conditions, or worn facilities.

- By staying engaged and ensuring a positive experience, you can build loyalty and encourage guests to return often.

PRINCIPLES OF SUCCESS

- **Embrace Change:** Things that don't change remain the same – things that stay the same become obsolete.

- **Measure Performance:** If performance is measured, performance improves. If performance is measured and reported back, improvement accelerates. – *Thomas S. Monson*

- **Results Matter:** People are paid to produce results, and results are the only measure of intentions.

- **Work Efficiency:** Work expands so as to fill the time available for its completion. – *Parkinson's Law*

- **Cleanliness Attracts Guests:** A clean restaurant attracts guests.

- **Profit as Capital's Wage:** Profit is the wage of capital, ensuring continued growth.

- **Path to Success:** Success comes from providing superior service, superior products, guest courtesy, enthusiastic staff, constant innovation, and leadership vision.

- **Attraction over Promotion:** Rely on attraction rather than promotion. Customers will sell your restaurant through word-of-mouth advertising. They speak favorably about you, return often, and bring others with them. The restaurant business is unique in that people like to share both their good and poor experiences.

-

"Most people are in favor of progress, it's the changes they don't like."

–Unknown

PRO-ACTIVITY SUMMARY BY STEVEN R. COVEY

The power, freedom, and ability to choose one's response might be called "proactivity." It might be called man's free will or agency, our inherent freedom to choose.

If we accept the fact that we are responsible, we must then accept that we may be judged as to whether we act responsibly or irresponsibly. Often, this judgment comes as a natural consequence of our behavior, for while we are free to choose our response, we are not free to choose the result of our response. Thus, we see that in the last analysis, our agency is the antecedent to the conditions of our lives. Agency is the basis of both our growth and our happiness and also our destruction and unhappiness. Psychologically, reactive behavior frees us from feeling responsible and gives us a false sense of security, but in reality, reactive behavior breeds insecurity and cheats us of true growth and happiness.

Proactive people focus on the inner circle of influence, and reactive people on the outer circle of concern. Proactive people do something about things they can control or influence. They generate positive energy, which feeds upon itself. As things get accomplished within the inner circle of influence, the circle gradually enlarges until it begins to encompass many of the concerns in the outer circle.

Reactive people generate negative energy, which also feeds upon itself. They neglect the inner circle of influence and worry about things over which they have no control. When we worry about things, we can do nothing about, that worry itself becomes part of the problem: opportunity is lost, day by day, because it's either not seen or not used. When we go to work on things, we can do something about, our industry becomes part of the solution. As the popular saying goes, "If we are not part of the solution, we are part of the problem."

We become Proactive through natural processes – through patience, persistence, and diligent practice. It is one of the great illusions of life to think that there is a simple formula, a quick fix, if we want to increase our level of pro-activity. In that case, we must exercise our patience and diligence, self-control and skill, improve our methods of influence, make deposits into other people's emotional bank accounts, listen with empathy, *and most importantly, fully accept the fact that we are responsible.*

HOW TO GROW YOUR RESTAURANT IDEAS

Your restaurant will grow if you understand the reasons for success and failure in the industry and commit to avoiding failure behaviors while fostering growth behaviors in yourself and your staff. Here's how to get started:

Understand Your Position: Know where you are today, where you want to go, and the gaps between the two. This understanding will help you determine what you must do today to close those gaps and realize your future potential.

Steps to Foster Growth

- **Read Trade Publications:** Learn from hospitality professionals and others in the industry about successful guest attraction strategies.

- **Stay Trend-Savvy:** Be aware of the types of food, service, and facility trends that guests may want in the future.

- **Eliminate Guest Frustrations:** Understand how eliminating frustrations can lead to your success.

- **Empathize with Guests:** Study, understand, and empathize with your guests to better put yourself in their shoes. Learn what makes them tick and how you would react to the experience you're providing.

- **Observe Usage:** Watch how people use your products, services, and facilities to learn what they like and dislike. Being both a guest and an operator requires training.

- **Read Body Language:** Pay attention to guests' body language and expressions. Empathy towards guests is crucial to being a guest-driven operator.

- **Study Other Operations:** Study different facilities, service processes, and food products to determine what guests expect and enjoy.

- **Listen to Feedback:** Listen to what guests, friends, and family say about their hospitality experiences.

- **Read Comment Cards:** Read guest comment cards and letters, both complaints and compliments, to understand what guests think about your hospitality.

- **Visit Other Restaurants:** Observe the conditions and guest experiences at other restaurants. Determine why people choose to eat there.

- **Self-Awareness:** Be aware of your own restaurant experiences; identify what you enjoy and what you don't.

- **Define Value:** Understand the definition of value and continuously work to increase the value you provide to guests.

- **Innovate:** Continually introduce and improve new products, services, and systems as guests' needs and wants change.

By implementing these steps and consistently striving to enhance your guests' experiences, you can foster growth and achieve long-term success for your restaurant.

MANAGING YOUR TIME
–TAKEN FROM THE GERBER E-MYTH MASTERY PROGRAM

Everyone gets 24 hours in a day, yet some people. Accomplish a great deal more in that day than others. Although most people rarely think of it this way, "time" is simply another word for "life." It's easy to see why good time management is critical. After all, you wouldn't let your staff, clients, vendors, and friends shorten the days of your life, so why are you letting them steal your time? Time is your single most precious resource, and it's one that only you can protect.

- ***Track the flow of your day.*** The first step is to understand how you currently spend your time. Use *a Daily Time Log* to track the flow of your time by logging everything you do throughout every day for two weeks. Don't be surprised if you find this tool so valuable. You'll want to continue using it as part of your ongoing time management system.

- ***Skim, Summarize, and Analyze how you use your time.*** When you have completed Daily Time Logs for two weeks, you will have enough information to provide a reliable understanding of your time management patterns. The best way to go about the analysis is to skim through all your Daily Time Logs to get a feel for the flow of your days. You'll see precisely what you do during the day and how long everything takes. You can expect some surprises, such as the time you spend on random phone calls, sales calls, social conversations, and other interruptions.

- ***Create your daily routine.*** Consider creating a Daily Routine, a pre-defined schedule for your typical workday, that maximizes the time you spend on productive work.

- ***Prioritize the flow of your day.*** A prioritization tool. 1) High priorities. 2) Secondary priorities 3) People you need to contact. 4) Telephone Call you want to remember. 5) Schedule a place to plan how and when you will accomplish your priorities for the day.

- ***Monitor your time management.*** You should periodically re-evaluate how you are spending your time, especially when you are breaking old habits and establishing new ones.

- ***Eliminate your time bandits.*** A time bandit is anything that steals your work time – a new staff member, a talkative vendor, the telephone, your wife or husband or broken equipment, etc.

- ***Organize and plan by identifying work items that could possibly be done today.*** Anything that improves your guest's experience should be done immediately. Break down long activities and projects into interim tasks.

- ***Prioritize and stay focused.*** Evaluate your list and prioritize items on your Daily Planner. Ask if nothing else gets done today. What are the one or two items that absolutely must be done? Hold five-minute meetings - Don't overbook; - Delegate – Routinize - Share time-saving ideas - Set deadlines - Take natural breaks – Close door, Work standing.

- ***Take care of unpleasant matters immediately.*** If you keep postponing them, they will haunt you and waste precious time reminding you they're still around.

- ***Use prime time for prime tasks.*** When are you at your best? Do important things that require lots of brain energy at that time. When your brain is frazzled, attend to minor things that don't take a lot of thought.

The bottom line comes down to your willingness and commitment to establish the habits that will give you more control over both the expected and the unexpected things that happen every day.

"The mastery of the art of leadership comes with the mastery of the self."

–James M. Houses and Barry Z Posner, authors of the book *"Leadership Begins with an Inner Journey"*

SUMMARY AND CONCLUSION

Implementing the principles in this book can minimize the need for advertising in the media, allowing you to operate a restaurant based on attraction rather than promotion. This requires presenting the restaurant experience attractively in every way for the enjoyment of your guests.

- **Understand Key Failures:** Recognize the primary reasons restaurants fail and the ten principles that govern guest loyalty and behavior. These insights are crucial for your success. If you aren't being successful look at the ten principles discussed in this book and discover where your restaurant is falling short. You must see these crucial factors from your guests' perspective.

- **Overcoming Location Challenges:** Effective operations can help you overcome a poor location. Guests will drive past many restaurants to find yours if you maintain high standards and offer more value and enjoyment than your competition.

- **Attention to Detail:** The devil is in the details. Be aware of all events and conditions that guests experience, both consciously and unconsciously. Develop systems to ensure positive and attractive guest enjoyment experiences consistently. Managers must know the details of each staff member's job to ensure they perform according to their position agreements and job descriptions.

- **Exceed Guest Expectations:** The primary aim of restaurants should be to exceed guest expectations in many ways and often. This book explains how to create loyal guests who prefer your restaurant over any competition.

- **Effective Operations:** Operating a restaurant effectively requires written systems and effective training so your staff members know exactly what to do and how to always do it. Several factors are vital in restaurant operations: facilities, services, and food products. Each element holds its importance and may appeal differently to guests.

- **Challenges of Putting Guests First:** There are challenges to always putting the guest first, including personnel management tasks, inventory, ordering, and maintenance issues. Position agreements, duty checklists, charts, and forms help people remember what needs to be done, how it's done, and when.

- **Proficiency in Personnel Management:** Being reasonably proficient in personnel management is necessary. Effective hiring, training, supervising, evaluating, and terminating hold staff performance and guest satisfaction together. Managing people can be rewarding and frustrating due to the different personalities you will hire.

- **Leadership and Guidance:** It's unlikely you will hire people who know how to run a restaurant and prioritize guests' interests all the time. You will need to lead and show them how to satisfy guests and ensure they return often, allowing your restaurant to thrive.

- **Financial Viability:** Lastly, you must operate profitably to support your family and your dreams of a great future. There is a danger in focusing on profit because it may lead you to forget about the ways you can lose customers. By providing the maximum guest enjoyment, you are likely to enjoy strong sales, which can provide a good profit.

- **Golden Profitability Factor:** *"Your Staff Members Must Hustle and Be Productive for You to Succeed. Hustle is profit because it produces faster service, which increases sales while reducing your staffing costs."*

- **Ingenious Hidden Treasure:** *Décor enhancements, when done effectively, can increase sales by as much as 30%. These enhancements can pay for themselves many times over a few years.*

SOURCES

Sam R. Lloyd - *Coaching Skills for Leaders: Helping Others Reach Their Potential.* Paperback December 13, 2005, by Crisp Publications, Inc.

Sharon Burke -- *Developing Positive Assertiveness, Third Edition: Practical Techniques for Personal Success. Paperback October 19, 2001, Crisp Publications, Inc.*

RMP - Restaurant Personnel Management April 9, 1990, Volume 6, No 6

Charles Coonradt - *The Game of Work: How to Enjoy Work as Much as Play.* Published July 19th, 2007, by Gibbs Smith

Utah Restaurant Association - *Crime Vulnerability Checklist*:

Dartnell Corporation - *Guests First, A Practical Guide to Profitable Customer Relations.* - 1997

Management Report - *Customer Service.* - April 9, 1997

Communication briefing - *Communication briefings.* Volume XVI No. II

Wayne R Pace - *Organization Vitality: The Fourth Agenda.* Brigham Young University.

Penton Corporation - *Nations Restaurant News*

National Restaurant Association - *Washington Weekly.*

Restaurant & Institutions. - *Toward Exemplary Service.* Bill Marvin

Centre for Strategic Management - *Creating Customer Value. Systems Thinking: "From Complexity . . . To simplicity"*

Disney Institute - *The Disney Keys to Management Excellence. Discover the Business Behind the Magic.*

Boardroom Reports - *Business Secrets.*

Utah Restaurant Association Publication - *Food for Thought.*

Foodservice Marketing Magazine.

National Restaurant Association. - *How To Invest In People - A handbook On Career Ladders.*

Humetrics incorporated - *Hire Tough Manage Easy Workbook – 1999*

James Allen - The Eight Pillars of Prosperity.

Lakewood Publications - *Total Quality Newsletter.*

Managing. - *The Entrepreneur's Guide to Success.*

Mortimer R. Feinberg, Ph.D. - *Management diversity strength.* Restaurant Business.

George Leonard Wenzel - *Wenzel's Menu Maker.* CBI Publishing, 1494 pages. 1966

Fenman Activity Pack. - *The manager as trainer, coach and guide.* Fenman Inc. 1999

Steven R. Covey - *Executive Excellence.* A monthly newsletter of personal excellence, managerial effectiveness and organizational productivity

Steven R Covey – *Seven Habits of Highly Effective People.*

Eileen M. Russo - *Supervisory Skills Questionnaire.*

Centre for Strategic Management. - *Creating Customer Value and Systems Thinking and Learning.*

CF & Y's, - *Foodservice information systems report*

Darnell Corporation - *The Effective Executive*

Eddie Davies - *The Manager as Trainer, Coach and Guide.* - Fenman,

Edie CohenLee and Sherman R Emery - *Dining By Design.* Cahners Publishing Company

Michael E Gerber - Gerber Business Development Corporation. - The E-Myth Academy, Modules 1-16

Michael E Gerber – INC Magazine. Why Do It All Yourself? Documenting Your Success - June 17, 2018

Michael E Gerber – *The E-myth Mastery.*

Migaly Csikszentmigalyi - *Finding Flow; The Psychology of Engagement with Everyday Life.*

Sam R. Lloyd - *Developing Positive Assertiveness Booklet.* A Fifty Minute Series Book. 1998

Jim Rohn – *The Treasury of Quotes.* - 1996

Jordan Peterson - *"12 Rules for Life"* an antidote to chaos.

Andrew Thomas - *The Secret Ratio That Proves Why Customer Reviews Are So Important:* Article in Inc. magazine.

Modern Restaurant Management - June 3, 2020

FsR magazine - April 2019

Wikipedia – *ISO 9000 and Kaizen articles.*

Tepper Kalmar Associates – Today's Restaurant Article

Nation's Restaurant News - March 9, 1987

Kevin R. Miller - *Customers Only Want Two Things*

ABOUT THE AUTHOR - A. GLEE ZUMBRENNEN

Owned and operated Brick Oven Restaurant in Provo, Utah

1962 to 2008.

Utah Valley Chapter of the International Food Services

Executive Association – Named Brick Oven Restaurant

- Restaurant of the Year - 1980

Utah State Chamber of Commerce Awards

- Utah's Outstanding Young Man 1978 (Jaycees)
- Total Citizen Award - 1980
- Outstanding Citizen in State of Utah - 1982

Utah Restaurant Association Awards

- Recipient of the Bronze Award - 2001
- Inducted in the Hall of Fame – 2018

www.ingramcontent.com/pod-product-compliance
Lightning Source LLC
Chambersburg PA
CBHW081814200326
41597CB00023B/4247